For Gher
from
Uncle and Aunt D. B. and Frances.

WILD BIRD NEIGHBORS

WILD BIRD NEIGHBORS

By
ALVIN M. PETERSON

THE BRUCE PUBLISHING COMPANY
MILWAUKEE

CONTENTS

WILD BIRD NEIGHBORS

Chapter 1

THE CUCKOO

MANY common birds are of more than passing interest and importance because they destroy insects in large numbers. The bobwhite and rose-breasted grosbeak are justly famous for the good work they do in destroying potato beetles; the flicker is fond of ants and devours them in large numbers; the bluebird and meadowlark not only eat many cutworms and grasshoppers, but also feed untold numbers to their young; and the swallow, the swift, and the nighthawk catch and destroy large numbers of flies, gnats, mosquitoes, and other pests while on the wing. Indeed, many insects seem to exist solely for the purpose of providing certain birds with food. If so, the tent caterpillar was created for the purpose of tickling the palates of cuckoos!

The cuckoo is a mysterious bird, more often heard than seen, shy, secretive, and suspicious. We hear its notes and know it is near, but rarely discover a sign of it. Often the bird we fail to see is in plain sight, concealed from our eyes by its protective colors. Sometimes, however, one is to be seen briefly as it flies off a short distance and vanishes from view again into some tree, bush, or thicket. Much less often one is found perched upon the branch of a tree, watching the intruder, crouching, tail drooping, as if ready for instant flight. Cuckoos are hard to see for several reasons: their light brownish plumage blends well with the surroundings; their flight is slow and winding; they glide silently from place to place; and they are experts at hiding among the leaves and branches.

There are several species of cuckoos to be found in the United States: the black-billed cuckoo, yellow-billed cuckoo, mangrove cuckoo, road runner or ground cuckoo, and groove-billed ani. The last three are not widely distributed, so it is with the former we are here mainly concerned, both being found in considerable numbers as far north as Southern Canada in summer.

The black- and yellow-billed cuckoos look so much alike that it is hard to tell them apart, unless you are near them. Both are brown above, white below, about 12 in. in length, and have long bills and tails. The former has a black beak, whereas the lower mandible of the latter is yellow. The latter also has a tinge of rufous about the wing feathers and its long, black tail feathers are heavily marked with white.

The nests of cuckoos resemble those of mourning doves, being frail and shallow and constructed largely of weeds and twigs. They are located in trees and bushes usually a short distance from the ground. The eggs are greenish-blue in color, and some nests contain both eggs and young birds in various stages of development at the same time. One of the first nests I ever found held one egg and two young birds.

However, it is the feeding habits of cuckoos that make them of most interest and importance to us, because they live largely upon caterpillars — especially destructive, spiny tent caterpillars. Many birds avoid this kind but cuckoos eat them as well as the smooth ones.

In my rambles through orchards, pastures, and woods, I frequently run across colonies of tent caterpillars that

Nest of tent caterpillar—cuckoos destroy these insects in large numbers.

sometimes do untold harm to the foliage of trees. I found the tent of an unusually large colony early in May one spring, took it home, and placed it in a screened cage on the porch for further observation. We found that the pests had escaped a few days later and wondered what had become of them. Soon we found out. All had made their way to the branch of a rosebush standing near the corner of the porch; they had eaten all the leaves and were busy building four new tents on it. I watched them for some time and soon discovered four crawling rapidly up the bush, one behind the other and nearly touching, as if trying their best to keep from becoming separated and lost.

The American tent caterpillar is the larva of a small, brownish moth that lays its eggs in belts about the twigs of orchard, shade, and other trees, but preferably about those of apple and cherry trees. Tiny caterpillars develop within the eggs and remain inside the shells over winter, being protected from the cold, rain, and enemies by a frothy, varnishlike material with which the shells are coated. They eat their way out the following spring, feast upon the varnishlike substance on the empty shells, then repair in a body to a suitable leafy twig or branch and there make a tiny silken tent in which to spend the nights and seek shelter from the cold, wind, and rain.

This tent has a hole or door which the caterpillars use when starting out to make a meal of the nearest leaves. All the caterpillars hatched from a batch or belt of eggs — two, three, or four hundred of them — make their home in the same tent, though when the leaves give out on one branch they travel to another and build a second, and perhaps larger tent there. The tiny, white, silken tent is their happy home and protects them from the cold, the rain, parasitic insects, and other enemies, but not from the sharp eyes and beaks of cuckoos!

Three or four hundred hungry caterpillars require a large amount of food and eat leaves by the hundreds and thousands, often taking enough to injure or kill a tree. They shed their skins from time to time and require food in ever larger quantities. They are nearly 2 in. in length when full grown, are covered with hairs or spines, and have a white stripe along the middle of the back.

Tent caterpillars change their ways when mature, scattering in all directions, finding their way to the ground, where they spin cocoons. The mature moths emerge from the cocoons in June and July and lay the eggs from which other caterpillars are hatched the following year.

However, few of the caterpillars live to spin cocoons if

there are cuckoos about, since the birds hunt up the tents, tear them open, and devour the pests by the hundreds. The contents of the stomachs of 46 black-billed cuckoos were examined at Washington and found to contain 906 caterpillars and many other pests. Likewise, 1,865 caterpillars were found in the stomachs of 109 yellow-billed cuckoos. One stomach contained 250 American tent caterpillars, which no doubt all but exterminated an entire colony.

I often hear cuckoos in our oak grove at night. Sometimes I hear them about trees near the house during the day, but, though I have frequently looked long and carefully, I still have my first cuckoo to see in the immediate vicinity. Those seen I find farther from home, mainly along the shores of a near-by stream, where many of the yellow-billed species nest. I once found a nest in a small red birch standing on the shores of a slough adjoining this stream on the west. A few days later we had a very heavy rain, and, when next I visited the spot, the tree and nest were under water, tragedy having overtaken the yellow-billed cuckoo's cradle.

There is a country road a half mile to the east of my home, that has a bank 8 or 10 ft. high on the west side. I was driving along this road one cool, bright July morning, when I discovered a nest in a young bur oak standing on the top of the bank. The nest was 3 or 4 ft. from the ground, next to the trunk, and was supported by three small branches. Apparently, the nest was an old discarded one, but nevertheless, I climbed the bank to inspect it, advancing cautiously from the south, stopping now and then for a better look, and saw there was a bird on the nest. I was sure it was a brown thrasher's nest I had found, judging from the first glimpse secured

Nest and eggs of the cuckoo.

of the bird, the nest, and the site, but found, upon getting nearer, that the occupant was larger than a thrasher and had a curved bill and that its color was a dull light brown and not reddish-brown. The bird was a cuckoo, which flew off after I had stood at a distance of 4 ft. and watched it for no little time. The nest, which had been made of leaves, twigs, weeds, and grasses, held a light greenish-blue egg about the size of a mourning dove's egg. Later on there were two eggs, but after that no more were laid.

Naturally, I was highly pleased over my find, especially since I was then particularly interested in securing pictures of the birds, and this nest was well located for photographic purposes. The bur oak was surrounded on the south, west, and north by young trees, bushes, and vines, which effectively screened one from the sharp eyes of the owners. Then, too, the oak stood in an open spot, permitting the sunlight to fall upon the nest and permitting the use of an umbrella blind. I decided to wait until the young birds arrived, however, before trying to secure pictures.

The eggs hatched sooner than expected, and the young birds were quite large before I got my first glimpse of them. I decided to try the umbrella blind first, placing it 4 ft. south of the nest. It now was eleven o'clock, about the right time of day, as the light for the next four or five hours would be in the right quarter for taking pictures.

Now began a long, long weary wait, during which I squatted or stood all humped up in my hot, cramped tent until I was nearly roasted. You have no idea of how hot and uncomfortable a small umbrella blind can be on a sultry summer day unless you have spent a few hours in one. To make matters worse, the adult birds were timid, suspicious, and sly and did not once go to the nest, upon which the camera was focused, though the mother again and again got within 2 ft. of it, just out of range of the machine. They hid behind leafy branches whenever possible, where they carefully watched the blind and continually uttered notes of alarm. "Er-cut-cut, er-cut-cut," they seemed to say, though this occasionally gave way to a low "coo-coo," or "koo-koo."

Finally, I removed the blind and set the camera beside the nest, intending to operate the shutter by means of a long string. I covered the machine as best I could with leaves and small leafy branches, hoping the birds would not be as afraid of this as they seemed to be of the umbrella blind. I waited until it was too late to secure a time exposure, for which I now had the camera set; but,

Young cuckoos make a pretty team.

though the birds hovered about the nest, even ceasing their notes of alarm, they failed to go to it.

I made a dummy camera the next morning, consisting of a small box about the size of the real camera, which I painted black and equipped with a bright can cover to represent the lens and shutter. For this I made a crude tripod. I set it 3 ft. from the nest, returned home, and waited four hours before going back to it. I now hoped to find that the birds had become accustomed to the dummy and that they would not be afraid of the real camera. I found the mother on the nest, shielding her young from the hot noonday sun, so approached her slowly and cautiously, set up the camera, and all but secured a picture before she flew off. I might have secured one had I had a longer-focused lens, so I could have worked a little farther from her. Nevertheless, I felt I had made a promising beginning, so removed the dummy, replaced it with the camera, and hoped she would soon return. This, however, she failed to do, though I remained in the vicinity much of the afternoon.

Finally, I was obliged to remove the camera and replace it with the dummy, leaving the latter set near the nest overnight. I arrived at the place shortly after noon the following day and ten minutes later had the camera set and carefully concealed with leaves and branches. Surely by now the cuckoos must have become accustomed to seeing a queer, black contraption set beside their nest! I looked at the nest after waiting an hour, but could see neither of the owners near it. I looked again an hour later and at last found the mother perched beside her nest. I was sure the moment for which I had waited so long had at last arrived, but the shutter failed to work and frightened the bird.

She was back, however, by four o'clock, perched in exactly the same place on one of the small branches beside the nest. I thought I heard the noise made by the released shutter, but gave the string an extra jerk to make sure an exposure would be made. The extra jerk proved too much for the timid bird and away she went, but I found that the exposure had been made and that I had one chance for a desirable negative. I quickly changed films, reset the shutter, and all but got a second picture before the watchful male discovered my hiding place and frightened the mother with his coarse "er-cut-cut" note of warning.

I spent five additional hours at the nest the following day, but failed to get any more pictures of the adult birds. I was surprised at this, for I was sure I would have little

A cuckoo beside her nest in a young bur oak.

trouble getting some extra ones of the mother, especially since she had ventured near the nest twice the previous day. Luckily, before setting the camera for the adult birds, I took a picture of the youngsters. Both sat as still as statues, but not until they had gotten as far from me as they could without falling out of the nest. They sat with their backs toward me, heads up, watching me, and made a pretty team.

I set the camera for the adult birds as soon as I had taken the picture of the youngsters, but though I waited and waited not a glimpse of the mother did I get. I soon learned the reason for this, for upon taking a better look at the nest I found that the stronger of the two young birds was missing. He had shown some signs of uneasiness once or twice before, as if he wanted to try his wings, and finally had been induced to leave by the parents. I saw no more of him or his mother. The male bird continued guarding the remaining bird without taking any chances himself, being careful not to go near the nest upon which the camera was focused. I could not help admiring his sharp eyes and cunning, though he did try my patience. He was sure to see me whenever I tried to learn how things were going at the nest, flying to a near-by post or tree and there, in an unconcerned way, preening his feathers, stopping just long enough from time to time to utter his warning "er-cut-cut, er-cut-cut." Plainly, he was telling his mate that I was still lurking about the vicinity and that she had better stay away.

I spent twenty-five hours or more about the nest of that pair of cuckoos, and, for my pains, secured two pictures, one of the young birds and another of the mother. However, I really got all I bargained for, the pictures and twenty-five hours in the open air. It was quite an adventure and from it I learned a thing or two about the character and habits of our shy, elusive, and secretive cuckoos.

Chapter 2

THE DOWNY AND HAIRY WOODPECKERS

TWO cheerful, industrious, and useful bird neighbors of ours are the downy and hairy woodpeckers, hardy bird carpenters dressed in black and white and seen winter and summer alike. They come to our trees and bird-food tray and feast upon insects and beef suet in the winter, while many of them nest about the wooded shores of a near-by stream in holes they make in willow, scarlet maple, red birch, and other trees in the summer.

Now, the chances are you have these likable birds for neighbors also, since they are to be found over the greater part of eastern North America. The downy usually is the more confiding and neighborly, whereas the hairy is more likely to be shy and retiring. Still, I am quite sure I see the latter fully as often as the former, though I do not succeed in getting as near to him, and he is more likely to protest against my intrusion with a loud "peek" note and to go bounding off to some other tree.

Often the first hint one gets that these birds are about is a tapping, sometimes low and muffled, again loud, sharp, rapid, coming from a near-by tree. If the notes are low, it is likely that they are looking for food or excavating nesting holes, whereas, if they are loud and rapidly delivered, the birds may be making springtime music. The birds hop up tree trunks and branches when looking for food, carefully examining the bark and wood, and occasionally hammering at trees to discover the where-abouts of pests living within them. Studies made by the United States Department of Agriculture indicate that from two thirds to three fourths of the food of downy and hairy woodpeckers consists of insects, chiefly harmful species, such as wood-boring beetles, grubs or caterpillars, and ants.

Woodpeckers cannot sing, but they have another way of making music, that of beating a lively "rat-a-tat-tat" on small dead branches, splinters, boards, and pieces of metal. They usually sit still for a short while and look around after drumming. Are they proud of their drumming and music? I should like to know, or are they trying to ascertain the effects of their efforts upon the ladies of the species, or upon rival drummers?

When you hear the drumming of a downy or hairy woodpecker, stop and look carefully along the trunks and branches from which the notes seem to come and you are likely to discover the drummer. If it is a hairy woodpecker, he will prove to be quite large, about 9 in. long, or slightly smaller than the robin; but, if it is a downy, he will be considerably smaller, only about 6 in. long, hardly as large as the bluebird. The males have red patches on the backs of their heads, otherwise the two sexes are dressed exactly alike.

The hairy woodpecker usually flies in an undulating or wavy way, and occasionally he calls "peek" as he flies along. The same note is used to indicate alarm or anger. The downy woodpecker also has a "peek" call note, but this is not as loud and sharp as that of the hairy, unless the downy is very much excited or alarmed. Consequently, the sharpness and loudness of this note is of some help in identifying them. A glance as to the size

A downy woodpecker at our suet stick.

assures the identification. A close examination shows that the downy's outer tail feathers are barred, while the hairy woodpecker's are pure white.

Woodpeckers have sharp, chisellike beaks which enable them to drill holes in the trunks and branches of trees. The hole may be a small one, just large enough to enable the bird to extract a grub or other pest, or it may be large enough to furnish it with shelter when the weather is cold and stormy, sleeping quarters, or a nesting place. The long, barbed, pointed tongues enable them to impale and dislodge the insect pests exposed by their stout, sharp bills. They nest in holes in trees, stubs, posts, and poles, and have four toes arranged in pairs, two in front and two behind, enabling them to grasp the bark or wood of trees firmly. They have stiff, pointed tail feathers with which they brace themselves as they hop up or rest on the trunks and branches of trees; and they travel head first up trees, but always back down.

The nesting holes of downy and hairy woodpeckers run horizontally into the wood a short distance, then curve downward and are enlarged at the lower end to make room for the eggs and the incubating bird. A few chips constitute the nest, and on these five pure-white eggs are usually laid, though the number may vary from three to six.

I once found a hairy woodpecker's nest in a willow which leaned out over a small stream, and often visited the vicinity after the stub held young birds. What a noisy family those woodpeckers had! The last time I passed that way the young birds were nearly full grown. I stopped the boat and awaited developments. Soon the mother returned from a foraging trip, edging toward the nesting hole little by little. She seemed quite excited and alarmed at seeing me, protesting against my presence with many loud, sharp "peek" notes. The youngsters heard her and began screeching at the tops of their voices as they crowded, jostled, and elbowed their comrades in an effort to reach the entrance hole, where they would be at the head of the bread line. The mother looked at me, then at her noisy family, scolded and sputtered with more "peek" notes, as much as to say: "Children, please be quiet. Can't you see we are being watched?"

There was another tall dead willow about 3 rods from this noisy nursery, near which a tree swallow was perched. I rapped loudly on the trunk and was surprised to see a swallow, the mate to the one perched near by, emerge from a hole near the top and a downy wood-

The hairy woodpecker.

pecker from another nearer the ground. I had found a
two-story bird apartment house this time, with tree swallows in the upper flat and downy woodpeckers in the
lower.

Another downy woodpecker had a nest in a willow
stub less than 80 rods away. The entrance hole was less
than 10 ft. from the ground, and what a neat entrance
it was, a perfect circle and just large enough to accommodate the owner. The mother often stuck her head out
when I visited the vicinity, though sometimes she failed
to do this until I rapped upon the stub to let her know
she had company. Sometimes I was obliged to rap two or

more times before she made her appearance and passed the time of day, or did she only try to say: "What, are you here again? Please do not disturb me, now."

The nesting holes downy woodpeckers make apparently are in demand by house wrens, bluebirds, and tree swallows. The latter are not blessed with stout, sharp beaks like the woodpeckers and nest in holes and crevices they find ready made. No doubt, the nesting holes of downy woodpeckers are more desirable than the larger ones made by hairy woodpeckers, redheaded woodpeckers, and flickers, since they are smaller and otherwise better suited to them. The first downy woodpecker's hole I ever found had been made in a stub about 12 ft. in height and 8 in. in diameter. The day I found the hole a bluebird was perched near it, sputtering and scolding and lamenting. I noticed the hole at once and assumed that the bluebird was alarmed because I was there. However, it seemed more angry than alarmed and hovered about the stub, scolding. Soon a downy woodpecker appeared in the entrance hole and then I realized what was up. Downy had made the hole and had a nest there, while the bluebird had later discovered it, noticed how desirable it was, and had decided to take possession of it only to find that the downy had not yet relinquished or discarded it.

Such comedies or tragedies — comedies to us, tragedies to the would-be tenants — are more numerous than many of us suspect. Another pair of downies had a nesting hole in a willow standing about a rod from the stream previously mentioned. The tree in which the hole was located was surrounded by other willows, some large, others small, and many crippled and deformed. The day I found the hole the mother downy was having

A flicker and redheaded woodpecker at the bird bath.

quite a time driving off three house wrens that had taken a liking to the hole she had made and were trying to deprive her of it. But the downy woodpecker was equal to the occasion. First, she drove off one wren, then another, and finally the third. She remained near the hole meanwhile, actually between it and the wrens, as if realizing she must keep the latter from getting to or taking possession of the prize. The wrens were very tame and often perched on branches 2 or 3 ft. from me. I wondered if the little rascals did this because they thought I would come to their aid. Rather, I suspect, they were so absorbed in the quarrel they did not notice me. Anyway, downy finally won out, and the wrens were forced to nest elsewhere, that is, two of them. It was these two wrens, I am sure, I later found nesting in a deformed willow about 2 rods distant. This willow stood at the edge of the water, and the nesting hole was less than 4 ft. from the ground. There they raised a family of five youngsters and liked the site so well that they used it for their second brood also. I was there the day the first young birds left the nest. Shortly afterwards the nest held another clutch of eggs.

Chapter 3

THE REDHEADED WOODPECKER

THERE are three birds I am likely to see any day in the year, provided the acorn crop is a good one. The first is the English sparrow, which formerly nested about the outbuildings, but now in our martin house, and which gleans food from the yard, barnyard, garden, and near-by fields. The second is the blue jay, which nests on the branches of our trees and gleans a living of waste grain, odds and ends it finds about the yard and barnyard, beef suet from our suet stick, and acorns it steals from the squirrels and woodpeckers. The third is the redheaded woodpecker, an erratic, hardy bird that lives upon acorns, insects it catches on the wing, and wood-boring beetles, grubs, and ants.

The redheaded woodpecker came near being our national bird. Just suppose the blue-black of its suit had been blue, then its colors would have been red, white, and blue, the exact colors of our flag. Indeed, because its colors somewhat approximate the colors of the United States flag, some folks call it the "Patriotic Bird" and "Flag Bird." Its head, neck, and upper breast are crimson, its wings and tail, blue-black and white, and its rump and underparts, white. It is nearly 10 in. long, not quite as large as the robin.

This thrifty, independent woodpecker is not as widely and uniformly distributed as many other birds, and it is somewhat erratic in its comings and goings. In some places it is among the most common of birds, whereas in others, sometimes but a short distance off, it may be very rare or entirely absent. It usually remains in a given place winter and summer alike, though occasionally, even where it is common, it is absent in winter. These rare winter absences, no doubt, are due to a scarcity of its favorite food.

The redheaded woodpecker is to be found in considerable numbers about open woods and pastures, where oak and beech trees are abundant. Oak trees usually have many dead branches, knots, knotholes, gashes in the trunk, and the like; and sometimes large branches are torn off by the wind, or a tree splits at a main crotch. For these and perhaps other reasons many oaks are more or less broken and crippled and are considered to be highly desirable by the redheaded woodpecker. About such trees it is able to find considerable animal food, excavate a nesting hole with ease, and find splinters and small dead branches suitable for drumming purposes. It usually is able to find large numbers of acorns beneath oaks in autumn also, choice food not to be overlooked.

Redheaded woodpeckers are quiet birds in winter, but toward spring they become noisy, screeching and beating lively drumming tunes on dry branches, loose boards, tin cans, pieces of sheet iron, the metal blades of windmills, poles, and what not. About the only note they utter in winter is a sharp "kit-ti, kit-ti, kit" when angry, alarmed, or excited. This note is also to be heard in the spring, summer, and autumn. They are especially noisy when courting, uttering a loud, harsh "charr-charr-rr-rr," which can be heard for some distance. There generally are two or more birds about at such times and all

Young redheaded woodpeckers.

screech loudly. Since there is no way of accounting for variations in the tastes of individuals, I sometimes wonder if the male birds with the strongest lungs do not secure the most desirable mates.

Things quiet down after the birds have found mates. Then you are likely to see and hear them excavating holes for their nests. I was sitting in the oak grove, resting, early in May, when I heard a dull tapping near me and discovered a redheaded woodpecker, no doubt a female, hard at work drilling a nesting hole. She seemed to have the hole about one third done, for she tilted rather far forward and hammered well inside the tree for a time, then bobbed back, looked my way, then tilted and hammered again. I happened to be sitting near the same spot one evening late in the month, when the mother came flying straight to the tree, alighted beside the entrance hole, bobbed or tilted forward as she looked inside. The bob or tilt became more pronounced each succeeding time until the front half of her body seemed to overbalance the rest, then inside she went. No doubt, she had been off getting her evening meal, for she now was busy incubating her eggs.

Trees containing the nests of redheaded woodpeckers are easily located after they hold young birds. The youngsters then screech and make much noise as they beg for the food brought by the parents. Rap or tap upon a tree, stub, or telephone pole containing a nest with young birds in it and the little fellows set up a great clamor, screeching and begging, since they think the noise is made by a parent.

Redheaded woodpeckers, naturally, are most frequently to be seen about the trunks and branches of trees looking for beetles, grubs, ants, and other insects, or acorns hidden in crotches, holes, cracks, and beneath splinters or loose bark. They also are frequently to be seen flying boldly from tree to tree, for they go up and down a given territory with considerable regularity, like a policeman on his beat. Sometimes they are to be seen clinging to the topmost branches, as if resting or doing some hard thinking.

After the first broods of young birds are safely out of the nest, redheaded woodpeckers again become noisy, no doubt because they are about to nest a second time.

Redheaded woodpeckers change their feeding habits in late summer, when they are to be seen daily catching insects on the wing, much like the phoebe, wood pewee, and kingbird. They perch quietly on the tops of posts, poles, stubs, and on the trunks and branches of trees, patiently waiting for insects to come flying their way. When they catch sight of a desirable pest, they dart or fly rapidly after it, turn abruptly this way and that, or make graceful loops in midair, often flying high and far before capturing their prey. They usually return to the original perching place as soon as the chase is over, where they eat the pest at their leisure before resuming their watching and waiting. These beautiful white, crimson, and blue-black woodpeckers are among the most useful of birds when thus engaged.

But redheaded woodpeckers are nearly as changeable as the weather. As soon as insects become scarce, and the acorns are ripe, they begin storing and living upon the latter. They are very thrifty, more so than blue jays and the white-breasted nuthatch, storing acorns in far larger quantities than they actually need. All autumn long I see them at work, early and late, gathering the nuts, now on the ground after an acorn, now on a post, stump, stub, or tree trunk hiding it in a crack or crevice. Crotches, nooks behind splinters, crannies beneath loose bark, cracks, and holes all are suitable places for storing nuts. These birds are not satisfied with the natural storage places at hand, making small holes in stumps, posts, stubs, and decayed wood in which to hide many others. One autumn I found a post that had been drilled full of small holes by redheaded woodpeckers. There were twenty-two holes in all on the south side where the wood was softest, which held twenty-five acorns. Most of the holes were just large enough to hold one acorn, although one held two and another three. About the same time I ran across an oak in the grove that had a gash 6 ft. long and 8 in. wide on one side. This gash was filled with partly decayed wood and was thickly dotted with small holes filled with acorns, there being nearly seventy of the nuts. Most of the nuts are stored with the shells on,

The thrifty woodpecker's storehouse.

although many are to be found with the shells removed;
and sometimes half nuts and half kernels are to be seen.

Our thrifty woodpecker does not succeeed in keeping
all the acorns he stores. The squirrels know, or find out,
about the stored nuts and do not hesitate to carry off
all they can or care for. And the blue jays help themselves whenever they find the woodpeckers off guard.

I frequently hear a great uproar in the grove or pasture
in late autumn and winter, the woodpeckers screeching
with all their might and flying wildly about as if dis-
tracted. On such occasions I usually see either squirrels
or jays near the woodpeckers, sometimes both. The
squirrels bark and growl as though they are the ones
being robbed, and the jays cry and fly about as if they

owned all the acorns stored in the neighborhood. The
woodpeckers are well able to guard their stores, screeching "kit-ti, kit-ti, kit," darting madly at a squirrel or
jay, and soon being joined by any other woodpeckers
living in the neighborhood. Eventually, the squirrels
and jays are only too glad to leave, although I doubt if
they ever leave before they have secured some of the
acorns stored in the vicinity. And I doubt, in spite of the
many raids made upon the storehouses of the woodpeckers by the jays and squirrels, if the redheads ever
go hungry. They have so many stores that if one is
robbed they fall back upon another not as yet discovered
by the thieves.

Chapter 4

THE FLICKER

"CUH, cuh, cuh, cuh, cuh" comes a loud ringing bird call from across the fields late in March. Then I know that the ceremonious flicker is back from points a short distance south, where it has been spending the winter.

Take a walk in the direction from which the notes seem to come and you may get a glimpse of the bird, provided you walk far enough, for the flicker has strong lungs and its call may be heard for 80 rods or more.

The flicker is a large brown woodpecker that helps the redheaded, downy, hairy, red-bellied, and yellow-bellied woodpeckers protect trees from the ravages of wood-boring beetles, grubs, ants, and other pests. It is to be found on the trunks and branches of trees, stubs, posts, and stumps when thus engaged. However, the flicker is frequently to be seen on the ground also, and then may be mistaken for the meadowlark, since both birds have black crescents on their breasts. But the meadowlark is chubbier than the flicker and has a yellow breast and white outer tail feathers. The flicker, on the other hand, has a white rump, a red patch on the back of the head, and its wings are lined with golden yellow. It is over 1 ft. long. Its most common note is its loud "cuh, cuh, cuh, cuh." Other common notes are its questioning "clape," its queer "wick-ee, wick-ee," and a low purring or chuckling note it utters as it bounds from place to place in a wavy sort of way.

The flicker is common and widely distributed and is known in different localities by dozens of odd names. Its notes are responsible for the names, clape and yarrup; its color and some other characteristics give it the following: yellow-shafted woodpecker, golden-winged woodpecker, yellow-hammer, and the like. Occasionally the flicker nests in a hole in the top of a tall stub, telephone pole, or high branch, which accounts for the names *high hole* and *high holder*. I frequently find nesting holes within 4 ft. of the ground, and a pair that nested in an old bur oak in the grove drilled the entrance hole 1 ft. from the ground.

Courtship is soon under way upon the return of the flickers in the spring, and then they are very queer indeed. Two of them are frequently to be found on poles, stumps, posts, tree trunks, and branches, facing each other, bowing, moving from side to side perhaps with mincing steps, swinging their heads from right to left, their wings and feathers quivering. The queerest thing about the whole performance is that when one moves and swings its head and the front part of its body in one direction, the other moves his in exactly the opposite. In other words, the birds seem to be out of step, or working entirely at cross-purposes.

The flicker is doing something of service to man when it is on the ground, as it frequently is. Sometimes one is to be seen hammering at the ground with its long, strong bill as it searches for a breakfast, lunch, or dinner of ants. It locates a spot where ants are numerous and there drills holes to reach their nests. The drilling excites the ants and they begin running in and out, here, there, and

A young flicker.

everywhere. That is what the flicker wants, and it at once licks them up with its long tongue.

Ants are interesting insects, but at times they prove harmful and annoying, making their way to cupboards and pantries and carrying off and polluting food, and thus forcing housewives to wage war upon them. But ants are harmful in another way also, as they have considerable to do with the comfort and spreading of a troublesome insect pest known as the aphis or plant louse. There are many species of plant lice, which infest trees, corn, melon, cucumber, and cabbage plants, roses, potted flowers, weeds, and many other plants, sucking the sap or life juices from them and either seriously injuring or killing them, sometimes laying waste acres upon acres of farm crops.

Plant lice are also known as ants' cows, since the ants secure a transparent fluid from them known as honey-

dew. Ants are fond of honeydew; consequently they
take good care of their cows, even carrying them from
plant to plant, or pasture to pasture, thus spreading
them in all directions. Furthermore, ants sometimes store
the eggs of aphids in their own nests over winter so
that they may be sure of having many cows the following
year. Ants, thus, are indirectly responsible for part of
the damage done by plant lice; and the flicker, when
destroying ants, is valuable to us, since it is helping
us keep the destructive aphids in check.

Stomach examinations made by the United States Department of Agriculture have shown that more than 50
per cent of the flicker's food consists of ants. "Of the
flickers' stomachs examined," writes F. E. L. Beal, "three
were completely filled with ants. Two of these contained
more than three thousand individuals each, while the
third contained fully five thousand. It is these insects for
which the flicker searches when it runs about in the
grass, although some grasshoppers also are taken."

The acorn crop was a failure in 1928, consequently
the redheaded woodpeckers left early in the fall and
did not return until the following spring. This led to
complications and war with the flickers.

The flickers arrived from the south late in March.
There were dozens of them, and two or three pairs spent
most of their time about the yard, pasture, and oak grove,
where, to all appearances, they intended nesting. There
was much bowing and "scraping" meanwhile, since
flickers are among the queerest of all birds when courting and nesting.

The flickers found and appropriated several of the
older and more crippled oaks in the grove and pasture.
Hence, the redheaded woodpeckers found them in full

A handsome young flicker.

possession of some of the more desirable trees and holes
when they arrived — trees and holes, by the way, in
which redheads had previously nested and which they
considered theirs because of previous occupation. Naturally, they were not to be deprived of them without a
struggle.

A pair of flickers took possession of an old hollow oak
near the barn. This oak had two holes in its trunk, one
of which the flickers appropriated, enlarged, changed,
and perhaps renovated. This hole was on the south side
and exactly 3 ft. from the ground by actual measurement.
A pair of redheaded woodpeckers tried to force the
flickers from this tree, or at least to allow the redheads
the use of the north hole. To this the flickers objected
and war followed. There was much noise, confusion,
quarreling, and fighting about the old oak for several
days after that as a consequence.

The flickers called "cuh, cuh, cuh, cuh" at the tops of
their voices, when the one or the other needed the help

of an absent mate; and the redheaded woodpeckers uttered their "kit-ti, kit-ti" and harsher "charr-charr-rr-rr" cries as they prepared to, or did, fight. One day I found a flicker and a redhead on the ground fighting it out with beaks and claws. The birds were fluttering and squirming on the ground, one, I could not tell which, having the other by the feathers of the neck. It was a real feather-pulling contest. Later the two stood up and faced each other, jumped up and down, dodged, struck at each other with feet and bills, much like two roosters. The flickers finally won out and the redheads were forced to nest elsewhere.

I chanced to pass the old oak about the middle of May and stuck my hand as far down the hole as I could. No sooner was my hand inside than I received a sharp peck that caused me to withdraw it in a hurry. My, but was I surprised! There sat the mother just inside the entrance, watching me, all ruffled up and very angry, ready to defend her nest against any and all intruders.

I visited the tree frequently after that, always rapping upon it to learn if she were at home. She nearly always came to the entrance when she heard me, looked sharply my way a few moments, then backed down into the nest again. Another large oak near the end of the pasture also was used that year by a pair of flickers for nesting. There, too, the mother became so tame and fearless she refused to leave her nest when I was near.

A little later I found that the nest in the first oak held young birds, since I could hear them screech. The mother now became more tame and fearless than ever, seldom, if ever, paying any attention to my visits. She never left the nest for a look at me from the entrance hole when I rapped on the tree. However, I always could tell whether

Young flickers.

she was at home or off securing food for her young, because when she was at home all was quiet within the tree, but, when she was absent, my rapping caused the youngsters to start screeching and begging for food.

The young birds left the nest shortly after the middle of June. We saw much of our handsome and useful bird neighbors during the remainder of the summer and autumn nevertheless, for they often hunted ants about the yard. They were well satisfied with their summer home, we judged, and were sleek, plump, and unafraid. The old oaks furnished them with nesting places, there was much food to be found about the pasture, grove, and yard, and they were not molested by enemies. Flickers ask no more and will continue nesting near you and faithfully serving you as long as such conditions prevail.

Chapter 5

THE NIGHTHAWK

YOU are more likely to see the nighthawk flying about in the evening than at any other time of the day, though it also is much on the wing on cloudy and rainy days, on bright, moonlight nights, and during the early morning hours. It is slightly larger than the robin and brown thrasher but appears considerably larger when flying because of the long, powerful wings which enable it to fly about for long periods of time. Its aerial evolutions are many and marvelous. Its feet, on the other hand, are weak and undeveloped for walking, running, or hopping, and when on the ground, the bird hobbles clumsily along.

It lives almost, if not wholly, upon insects it catches with its wide mouth as it skims along so gracefully: ants, June bugs, dung and click beetles, weevils, butterflies, moths, flies, grasshoppers, mosquitoes, potato beetles, cucumber beetles, bill bugs, bark beetles, squash bugs, and many others. Scientists have found as many as fifty species of insects in a single stomach, whereas "the number of individuals ran into thousands."

The nighthawk returns to its breeding grounds about the middle of May, when summer is near at hand and winged insects are abundant everywhere. The first hint one usually gets that the bird is back is the sound of its nasal "peezp," "peeg," or "peent." Look high above you when you hear this call and you should catch sight of one or more circling and sailing almost out of sight.

Soon courtship, mating, and nesting are under way and then you should have little trouble hearing the night-hawk's booming or zooming. The bird first flaps his wings vigorously when flying, then sails or shoots this way and that with them held widespread and motionless; and it utters its nasal "peezp" during each series of wing beats. Does the exertion help liberate the sound? I should like to know. The male often thus flaps his wings, calls "peezp," and shoots upward, climbing ever higher and higher in the sky, then turns and swoops downward at a terrific speed until near the ground, or the tops of the trees, where he turns sharply with a loud zooming sound. The bird seems proud of his ability to make this sound and, at times, accidentally or otherwise, seems to enjoy "booming" near a person's head. This sound, no doubt, is made by the air rushing swiftly by or through the wings, much as a humming sound is produced when a stick, attached to a string, is whirled rapidly about. The male booms when courting and thus tries to make a favorable impression upon the lady of his choice; and, with this loud sound, he later entertains her when she is sitting most soberly upon her eggs. The booming thus takes the place of the drumming of the ruffed grouse and woodpeckers, and the songs of songbirds.

Should you chance to see a bird sitting lengthwise the branch of a tree, not crosswise like most birds, you may be reasonably sure you see a nighthawk. You will have little trouble getting near it at such times as a rule, since it is resting and does not wish to be disturbed. The white bars on the bird's wings serve as another aid in identifi-

A winking nighthawk on her eggs.

cation and usually can be seen as it perches. Nighthawks seem to me to be wise birds when thus resting — at least they look that way — for they sit with their eyes nearly closed and move their heads very, very slowly as they follow your movements. They seem to know they are safely out of reach, whether you are dangerous or not, and are ever ready to make the right move when action is demanded.

The nighthawk builds no nest, but lays its eggs in a slight depression in the ground, among leaves and chips, on a flat rock, or the graveled roof of a city building. The eggs match their surroundings in color and are hard to see; the same is true of the sitting mother and the young birds after they arrive. One sometimes is obliged to stand for some time, carefully examining the ground inch by inch, when trying to discover a sitting bird, or her eggs or young, of whose approximate location one is well aware. You can usually get quite near without dis-

turbing her, for she relies upon her protective colors and
remains quietly on her eggs or young as you pass. Stop,
look, and point her way and she usually flies off, as she
knows she has been discovered.

I once found a nighthawk sitting on her two mottled
gray-and-brown eggs on a sandy knoll a short distance
from the house. We often visited the spot and the mother
eventually became so tame that she allowed us to stand
at a distance of 4 ft. and watch her. The eggs hatched
early in July and we went to see the young birds. The
next time I passed the spot the mother and young birds
were missing; and, a day or two later, I ran across a pair
of nighthawks on a near-by knoll. I had passed the second
knoll dozens of times previously without discovering a
nest, so was quite sure that the birds that so mysteriously
disappeared from the first knoll were the very ones I now
found on the second.

How did the young birds manage to get from the first
to the second knoll? Did the mother carry them? I think
not. Rather, I think they made the journey afoot. True,
nighthawks cannot run or hop briskly, but they can
hobble or toddle slowly. The mother no doubt led the
way and urged her youngsters on, while they toddled
after and little by little made the journey safely.

The mother threw herself on the ground near my feet
and seemed to be badly injured; nevertheless, she
managed to keep well out of reach, feebly flapping her
outstretched wings, fluttering, gasping, occasionally saying "quit," and carefully watching me. I knew she was
feigning injury and that she was trying her best to lead
me as far as possible from the young birds. The male
sat on a dead branch just above my head and there acted
as if he were as badly injured as the mother. Sometimes

The eggs of the nighthawk who never builds a nest.

he hobbled slowly and clumsily along the branch with spread wings and gasped as though in great distress. I followed the mother, allowing her to lead me far down the pasture. There she miraculously recovered, flew gracefully off, circled, and headed back toward her young.

I flushed a nighthawk from a bare spot near an oak a year later and found she had been covering a tiny young bird and an unhatched egg. I placed an umbrella blind near this "nest," since I wished to secure a picture of an incubating or brooding nighthawk. The second egg hatched while I was waiting for the mother to return. I waited for a long time, but the solicitous parent did not return to her youngsters, though she often flew over the spot, even settled on the ground a few feet from it, so I eventually left without securing the desired shot. I did not dare keep the mother away too long for fear the young birds might perish from hunger and exposure. That night mother and young were still there, but the following day they were missing.

I found another "nest" (What else can I call it?) about a quarter of a mile off, which held one egg. The other egg had been punctured in some way, having a neat, circular hole in the shell, and had been rolled aside, where its contents had partly evaporated and baked in the hot sunshine. I visited the spot after the remaining egg hatched and secured a picture of the tiny youngster. This proved too much for the parents, and, the following day, I found the little chap about a rod off. I took a second picture of it and then left. The next day I found that the parents had decided to take no more chances, for I failed to find a trace of them or the youngster.

I located another "nest" on a bare spot between some oaks in the pasture, which held one egg. Shortly afterwards a second egg was laid and then incubation began. I spent considerable time in the vicinity, and the mother eventually became so fearless as to allow me to stand near her without showing any sign of alarm or flying off. Still, I had a hard time getting pictures of her. I first tried setting the camera near the eggs, hoping the bird would return and that I could make the exposure by means of a long string I had fastened to the shutter. The bird, however, was afraid of the camera and did not resume incubating, though she often flew over or settled upon the ground near her eggs.

I next tried introducing the apparatus gradually. First, I drove a stake into the ground about 3 ft. from the eggs; this was needed for operating the shutter. Next, the camera was set about 7 ft. from them, to which the bird soon returned. The camera was now set 4 ft. from the

A newly hatched nighthawk.

eggs, and the mother again resumed incubation without any fussing and loss of time. The camera was moved forward again, this time to a spot from which an excellent picture could be secured, but now the mother failed to return.

I placed an umbrella blind 4 ft. from the eggs the following morning, hid behind a tree, and awaited results. She soon returned to her eggs, so I secured the camera, took two companions with me, and, with them standing conspicuously beside the eggs, entered the blind, set up the machine, and then had them walk slowly off. The nighthawk was thus made to think that no one remained behind. The ruse worked, and the bird, without any preliminary flying about the vicinity, alighted upon the ground near the eggs and waddled to them. She turned

Young nighthawks, just out of the shell,
are queer little fellows.

around, made some adjustments of the feet, then settled down, enabling me to secure an exposure. Not a move did she make as the shutter clicked again and again and three additional pictures were secured. I now removed the machine, setting it outside the blind on the far side, then crawled forth from my hiding place — out the back door, as it were — walked to one side for a parting look, and found she still was contentedly dozing in the sunshine.

I found a nighthawk perching on the railing of our back porch one September afternoon that autumn. The bird evidently was very sleepy and tired, for it sat with its eyes closed and did not offer to make a move. I watched it for some time, then decided to try to secure a picture. I secured and set up the camera, working very slowly and cautiously so as not to frighten the bird, making two exposures before moving the camera 2 ft. nearer. The camera now stood less than 4 ft. from the sleepy-looking bird, and not a move had it made meanwhile, though the eyes were opened to mere slits a few times while I was adjusting the camera a second time. I took two additional pictures and then removed the machine without disturbing the tired bird. No doubt it succeeded in getting a good rest before it finally left.

I secured pictures of a third nighthawk in much the same way two years later. This bird was sitting on a pile of lumber, over which a piece of roofing had been thrown to protect it from the sun and rain. This bird also seemed to be very sleepy and tired and allowed me to take several pictures of it without showing any signs of alarm or flying off. It watched me much like the one perched on the railing of the porch, opening the eyes to mere slits, otherwise not a move did it make.

Chapter 6

THE WOOD PEWEE

"PEE-e-wee, pee-e-wee, pee-ah-way" comes a plaintive bird song from the oak grove late in May, telling me the wood pewee is back for a brief summer stay. I find him perched on a branch, moving his head continually, looking up, down, and from side to side, ever on the watch for the winged pests which he catches by means of short, darting flights. Pewee's song is but a repetition of his name, the first renditions having a rising inflection, the latter a falling, as if our bird is very tired and through singing for the day. But, no, there the song is again after a brief pause, much as before, for this flycatcher is to be heard off and on all day long.

The wood pewee is a near relative of the phoebe, common kingbird, Arkansas kingbird, chebec or least flycatcher, olive-sided flycatcher, and crested flycatcher, all of which are more or less fearless and pugnacious. The common kingbird is famous for the way it attacks and drives off hawks and crows, birds many times its size. However, the pewee is fully as fearless and pugnacious as the kingbird, attacking and putting to flight blue jays, redheaded woodpeckers, and even nighthawks, but paying little or no attention to small birds like warblers, wrens, and goldfinches.

A pair of pewees built a nest in the grove one sum-

mer, not far from the nesting hole of a pair of woodpeckers. The nest was located far out on a branch 25 ft.
from the ground, being a neat, artistic creation of grass
and fibers, shallow, but ornamented with lichens and
saddled to the limb. The young woodpeckers left the nest
about the time the pewees were building, and the parents

The fearless pewee.

led them off among the trees until they reached some
oaks in the pasture, where they afterwards spent much
of their time. The young woodpeckers and their parents
frequently returned to the grove, however, to forage and
pay their old home a visit perhaps, only to be more or
less annoyed by the pewees. The woodpeckers were no
match for the pewees and took refuge behind the trunks
of trees, where the latter took turns at darting at them,
forcing them from one to another until the larger birds
were well outside of what the smaller considered their
domain. The woodpeckers were belligerent enough when
a pair of bluebirds tried to nest in a near-by post, tormenting the latter until they deserted the vicinity and built in
a bur oak far down the pasture. Thus, the woodpeckers
fought and conquered the bluebirds, but were put to

shameful flight by the fearless little pewees. Occasionally
a nighthawk or blue jay also blundered into the grove
and were driven off by the pewees. The nighthawk did
not leave a step at a time like the woodpeckers, but took
to its wings and made its escape with a single mad dash.

I took several pictures of the young pewees when they
were about half grown, a task that entailed considerable
engineering, since it is not an easy matter to photograph
young birds in a nest far out upon a small oak branch
25 ft. from the ground, especially when there are no limbs
beneath the one on which the cradle is located. Fortunately, there was a larger branch just above the one on
which the nest had been built. I secured a tall ladder, a
long rope, and two stout straps, climbed the tree, and
tied the rope to the nest branch with a loose knot. I next
poked the knot as far out along the branch as I could,
threw the loose end of the rope over the upper branch,
and tied the latter to a third branch near me. I then cut
the branch on which the nest was located, which was
kept from crashing to the ground by the rope, making
the cut about 2 ft. from the trunk so I would have a stub
to which to strap the severed member. I grasped the near
end of the cut branch, thus keeping it from twisting and
turning end for end and dumping the young birds to the
ground, pulled it toward me, and strapped it securely
to the stub. The artistic cradle and young birds were now
about 4 ft. from the trunk, whereas before they had been
8 or 10. Now it was an easy matter to strap or tie the
camera to the trunk and take the pictures.

The most fearless pewee I ever met I found living about
a neighbor's oak grove which served as a windbreak for
the orchard, and was located on the south and east slopes
of a small rolling hill. I frequently visited these places,

The nest and young of the wood pewee.

and, when I did, nearly always heard his plaintive "pee-e-wee, pee-e-wee, pee-ah-way" and saw him as he darted from some perch and caught an unsuspecting insect. He returned to his perch and there devoured the captured morsel at his leisure.

One day when wandering about the grove, which he seemed to consider his domain, I found him perched upon the small, dead, lower branch of an oak. I turned and walked toward him until I was only a few feet away, fully expecting he would become alarmed and dash off. Imagine my surprise, when he darted toward me and caught an insect within a few inches of me. A minute later he almost brushed against me as he flew swiftly by, eager, intent, bent upon capturing an insect I frightened from the grass. I soon found I could walk near the post or branch upon which he was perched without disturbing him, that he paid no attention to me whatever, but was eagerly watching for the insects I frightened from the grass whenever I moved. Once he flew off for some distance, caught an insect, then returned to the post from which he started; near this I still was standing.

I returned to the grove in the afternoon with the camera, hoping to get a picture or two of my fearless little friend. I heard his notes as I approached the orchard and found him perched on a fence post. He had changed perches three or four times before I overtook him, for he was always busy and on the go. I followed him about for two hours, setting up the camera, focusing it, adjusting the shutter and film-pack adapter, and then, if no insect appeared in sight, causing him to move, making an exposure. I sometimes encouraged him to move to a more suitable perch by slowly poking the tripod toward him, sometimes getting it within inches of him before he darted from me and snapped up an insect. To all appearances, the insect and not the tripod caused him to move. All of his actions were perfectly natural. I could have caught him several times, I am quite sure, had I cared to. Once he flew to the top of a tree, where he rested and preened his feathers; and twice he flew off for longer distances. However, I soon heard his plaintive "pee-e-wee," as if he were calling me, and I shortly overtook him again.

I had many excellent opportunities for observing the bird's size and plumage. It is a little over 6 in. in length, rather slender of build, and gray in color. The feathers on the crown are dark gray; the nape, back, rump, and tail are somewhat lighter; and the wing feathers are edged with light gray, giving the bird prominent wing bars. The pewee is much lighter underneath than above, being lightest on the throat, slightly darker on the breast, and then lighter again on the underparts. The bird often seems sleepy and unmindful of what is going on about

The nest and young of the wood pewee.

it, whereas just the opposite is true. The mandibles do not move when the bird sings and are held less than ¼ in. apart.

My fearless little friend was exceedingly hungry three mornings later, when I found him in his favorite haunts and secured two additional pictures of him. Three moths and a score of other insects were devoured by the bird during the short time I followed him. I secured the pictures when he flew to the top of a post, fluffed out his feathers, and settled down for a rest or nap in the sun.

Three times during the morning he stopped feeding long enough to put other birds to flight. The first bird forced to scurry was a Baltimore oriole he discovered in a bur oak. The pewee darted for the oriole like a flash, and the two birds dodged and fluttered among the leaves and branches for a few moments, after which the oriole dashed to the top of a tall black oak with the little pewee in hot pursuit. There the chase continued, the birds darting from place to place, the oriole in the lead, the pewee madly following. Finally, there was a brief silence followed by the pewee's whistled song. The chase was over, the oriole either having dashed off or found a safe hiding place. The second was a downy woodpecker hopping up and around a fence post, which the pewee attacked though he was obliged to fly 2 rods out of his way to do so, while the third was either a goldfinch or vireo, most likely the latter.

Thus that little pewee spent the day, feeding, singing, resting, sunning himself, preening his feathers, and putting other birds to flight, each as the humor seized him. Wide awake, an expert flier, confident, unafraid, aggressive, surely he was a fearless pewee.

Chapter 7

THE KINGBIRD

THE flycatcher family, to which the fearless pewee and the common kingbird belong, is highly useful to man, because the species and individuals of which it is composed are experts at catching mosquitoes, flies, ants, beetles, and other small pests on the wing. These birds choose perches that give them an unobstructed view of their surroundings, wait patiently for insects to fly their way, and then catch them by means of darting flights. They have sharp eyes, broad bills, wide mouths, and strong wings which enable them to catch insects quickly and easily, often with audible clicks of their beaks. Flycatchers, on the whole, are small birds, and all are dressed in gray and brown, though their suits may be trimmed with yellow or white.

One of the most famous and handsome of the flycatchers is the common kingbird. It is about 8 in. in length, 2 in. shorter than the robin, and is grayish black above but white on the breast and underparts. It has a white bar or stripe across the end of the tail, and this is the field mark by means of which it may best be identified. The kingbird is always more or less noisy and active, screeching, flying boldly from place to place, darting after insects, moving its head freely even when perched on a post or branch, and keeping a watchful eye over its surroundings.

A kingbird and redheaded woodpecker
at the bird bath.

The kingbird is also known as the tyrant flycatcher, because it often wages war upon other birds, both large and small, and drives them out of the neighborhood in which it lives and builds its nest. However, many folks consider the kingbird to be brave and not a tyrant, since it defends its nest, eggs, and young with skill and daring, and does not molest birds of which it has nothing to fear and which do not invade what it considers to be its territory. All birds do their best to keep other birds from their nests, and some birds are among the worst enemies of other birds. Bluebirds have been known to drive field and chipping sparrows from the neighborhood of their nests, and robins to do the same with house wrens, and these birds are neither cowards nor bullies for doing so. That kingbirds are brave and fearless is shown by the way they attack and drive off hawks and crows, birds many times their size. They are sure to see a hawk or crow getting near the nest, to pounce upon it, and force it to fly off, the smaller birds taking turns at darting for the enemy, striking it with their beaks, alighting on its back perhaps, and tormenting it until it is glad to hurry off.

I once saw two kingbirds drive off four crows. The two birds flew rapidly toward each other after driving off these hereditary enemies as if mutual congratulations were in order. The two flew rapidly upward, then shot downward again at a great rate of speed, the distance between them hardly varying during the performance. No doubt this was their way of showing how happy they were over the outcome of the adventure. Sometimes a kingbird flies straight upward, spirals and turns sharply here and there, turns a somersault or two, and chatters and screeches as though out of its wits. The bird may be chasing a nimble insect, or trying to make a favorable impression upon its mate, or securing some needed exercise. Speediness of flight, brave hearts, and the ability to twist, turn, and dodge, make kingbirds great insect destroyers as well as terrors to hawks, crows, and other enemies.

The kingbird has been further slandered by being called the bee martin and bee bird and accused of catching and eating honeybees and thus doing some damage to the beekeeper. The kingbird does little harm to the beekeeper, however, and, on the whole, is a useful bird. The contents of the stomachs of 655 kingbirds were examined by the Biological Survey at Washington, where it was learned that only 22 of the 655 had eaten bees. Sixty-one honeybees in all were found and of these 51 were useless drones, not useful workers. Kingbirds know a thing or

Young kingbirds with their white vests are
handsome young fellows.

two and take the drones in preference to the workers,
since the latter have stings and the former have not. They
also have little trouble telling the latter from the former,
because the drones are much the larger. On the other
hand, kingbirds destroy many robber flies, that sometimes do considerable damage by taking honeybees, more
than offsetting the harm they may do by taking an occasional worker bee. From 80 to 90 per cent of the kingbird's food consists of insects, mostly injurious species.

Another kingbird, the Arkansas kingbird, lives west of
the Mississippi River. It is about 1 in. longer than the
common kingbird and may be recognized by its white
outer tail feathers. This bird is noisy like its eastern
cousin, but useful, nevertheless. It loves to perch on the
topmost twig of a tall tree and to dart after winged pests
for food. The notes of kingbirds are hard to describe, but

once known are easily recognizable. Some of the notes of the common kingbird sound like the noise made when a pair of shears is rapidly opened and closed, while another may be written "tseep." Some of the notes of the Arkansas kingbird are so loud they may be heard for a long distance, and they often are uttered when the bird is in pursuit of some insect. Thirty bees were found in the stomachs of 62 Arkansas kingbirds, and of these 29 were drones!

The common kingbird returns from its winter home in Central and South America early in May and for the next three months is much in evidence. It usually nests on the branches of trees, sometimes near the top, again much farther down, building a bulky cradle of twigs, weeds, grass, paper, rags, string, and other materials and lining it with fibers, rootlets, fine grass, wool, down, and the like.

Hunting for the nests of birds is considerable sport, and one of the things that makes it exciting and interesting is that nests are often found in unusual locations. Birds of a given species generally nest in places that are somewhat alike. Thus, vesper sparrows always nest on the ground, in tufts of weeds and grass, beside humps and clods, and in hills of corn, beans, potatoes, and other plants; catbirds prefer small, bushy trees and tangles; brown thrashers like bushes, brush piles, and the lower branches of trees; and bluebirds nearly always select holes in trees, posts, stubs, and stumps.

I nearly always run across a few nests each year that have been built in queer places. For example, I sometimes find the nests of robins, brown thrashers, and mourning doves on the ground. One such robin's nest had been built on the ground in an old field, in a patch of bush clover.

This partly submerged willow was used by a pair
of kingbirds for a nesting site.

Grackles usually build in crotches and on the branches
of trees near water, but sometimes a nest is to be found
in a hole in a tree; and I once found a bluebird's nest in
the end of a splintered beam in the end of a boxcar,
where, to all appearances, a coupler had been pulled out.

While kingbirds usually nest on the branches of trees,
they sometimes select rather odd locations. H. K. Job, in
his book *The Sport of Bird Study,* tells of finding a nest
on the top of a fence post, where he secured some excellent pictures of the cradle and its owners. Two kingbirds' nests I once found were located in much more
precarious places, though not in as advantageous ones
from a photographic standpoint. The first had been built

The kingbird's nest in the partly submerged willow.

on the trunk of a red birch that had toppled headlong into a large neighboring stream. The bank was about 8 ft. high at that point, and, near the brink of the bank, the birch had stood proudly for years, since it was quite large and had a trunk more than 1 ft. in diameter. The bank was at a bend, where the current had undermined the tree and caused it to fall into the water; and, upon the trunk, about two thirds the distance from the base to the top, the kingbirds had built, about 6 ft. from the swirling surface of the stream. The nest was made of twigs and string mainly, and great tangles of the latter material dangled from it.

I found the second a few years ago when visiting a county park located along the banks of a smaller stream.

A kingbird was perched in a willow, chattering and scolding as if it had a nest near by, but, though we carefully examined the near-by trees, we could not find it. We returned to the stream eventually, to inspect some bank-swallow holes in which several of these birds were nesting. There was a young willow lying in the stream partly submerged by water but still alive and partly covered with leaves. Strangely enough, there was a nest on the partly submerged willow, and, in the nest sat a kingbird. She seemed quite tame, no doubt because she had seen many folk about the park, and remained where she was, though we stood only 8 or 10 ft. away and watched her. Here, then, was the reason for the chattering, scolding, and alarm of the male kingbird we found perched in the other willow. The willow was about 6 ft. from the shore, and the nest less than 2 ft. from the water. We did not disturb the bird on the nest, though later we found her absent and noticed that the cradle held eggs, two being visible from the bank.

Chapter 8

CROWS AND HAWKS

SEVERAL boy scouts and I spent many glorious days during the spring a few years ago along the freight branch of a railroad. We called the place we liked best the "Boxcars." This was a marshy spot ½ mile long that bordered the railway on either side and was located about 4 miles west of the city limits. There were four or more side tracks at this point, upon which a few hundred, old, dilapidated boxcars stood. Nearly all of them had been in wrecks and were more or less crippled; some of them apparently had stood there for years and made excellent nesting places for birds that like a roof over their heads. Barn swallows and phoebes nested about the rafters of the cars, or upon ledges along the walls; a pair of bluebirds had a nest in the end of a splintered beam at the end of one; a pair of robins had their cradle above a grease box, while another had built one upon a suitable inside ledge; and some noisy English sparrows had a mass of rubbish above a side door, just beneath the eaves of another.

Crows nested in an oak grove on a hill 30 rods northwest of the siding; bitterns thundered from a marsh south of it; and sandpipers and killdeer ran about the shores of several ponds in the vicinity. A pair of mourning doves had a nest on the top rail of an old fence southwest of the "Boxcars"; at least four pairs of wrens

The Boxcars.

had their cradles in holes in posts near the tracks; and
more than a dozen pairs of blackbirds had built in a large
marsh that nearly surrounded the larger of the ponds.
King rails, catbirds, song sparrows, swamp sparrows, and
flickers also nested in this bird paradise. We found three
song sparrows', two swamp sparrows', a flicker's, a king
rail's, and more than a dozen catbirds' nests.

There was a large swampy thicket southeast of the siding, in which catbirds, yellow warblers, mourning doves,
Wilson's thrushes, rose-breasted grosbeaks, and green
herons nested, some of them in considerable numbers.
North of this thicket, across the tracks, there was a marsh
and a number of ponds. Here king and sora rails, green
herons, and American bitterns were frequently to be seen.
Elsewhere, near by, we saw marsh wrens, yellowlegs,
and woodcocks.

Early in the spring the boy scouts and I discovered a

crow's nest in a shapely white oak that stood on the south slope of the wooded hill northwest of the ponds and sidings. We could just see the mother's tail, which we at first mistook for a stick, as she was crouching in her nest. We rapped sharply on the trunk with a stick, and the sitting bird bounded almost straight upward, uttered a startled "caw, caw," and flew off. One of the boys climbed the tree and, from his breezy perch 35 ft. from the ground, told us the nest held young crows. He commented on the red-flannel lining of the mouths of the youngsters and noticed that the nest was lined with grapevine bark.

We returned to this nest a few days later to get some pictures and so had a camera, a long rope, and a basket with us. One of the boys climbed the tree, taking the rope and basket with him. He deposited the young crows in the basket when he reached the nest, and lowered the youngsters to the ground. Here the rest of us photographed and studied them as much as we wished, then replaced them in the basket for the return journey to the nest.

The young crows were too small and awkward at this time to photograph to advantage. Their half-naked bodies, large heads and mouths, and ungainly stomachs made them look ugly, and they were not able to perch satisfactorily upon the branches on which we placed them. Consequently we made a third journey to the nest when the youngsters were nearly large enough to leave their oak-tree home. Joe again climbed the tree, this time with a rope and a sack. One of the young crows flew off as he climbed the tree, but the others remained in the nest, where, in spite of protesting "caws," they were deposited in the sack and lowered to the ground.

The nest and eggs of a king rail.

There we placed them on stumps, logs, and branches and took their pictures. This time they proved excellent subjects, and we photographed them again and again in any number of poses, then replaced them in their sack elevator, in which they safely reached the nest.

Many young birds are hard to handle when taken from the nest. They scratch, peck, hop or run off, and refuse to pose for pictures. But not so these young crows. They quieted down after we had petted them a few minutes and acted as if nothing unusual were taking place. We admired their bright eyes and glossy black suits. How could a crow mother help loving them! We found them gentle and attractive, fully as likable as the youngsters of birds with much better reputations. And they were safe as far as we were concerned. We would no more have thought of harming them than we would have

Young crows in their shiny black suits.

thought of destroying young bluebirds, song sparrows, or wood thrushes.

I found another crow's nest sometime later that also held young ones that were large and handsome and suitable for the taking of pictures. I started climbing the oak in which the nest was located and had nearly reached the bulky cradle when the young birds began cawing and hopping from it. First one hopped out along a large branch and flew off, then another, and finally the third and last. However, they were not able to fly far and we soon overtook them. We cornered and captured all three, perched them in a row on a fallen branch, and then and there I secured my best crow pictures. To be sure, an obstreperous fellow occasionally flew off a few yards, but we caught him again and returned him to the branch. All told they posed as nicely and often as one could wish; and the pictures secured were very good, since the youngsters were fully fledged and about as large and handsome as crows ever get.

The wooded hill northwest of the "Boxcars" produced another nest in which the same boy scouts and I became greatly interested, no doubt that of a pair of red-shouldered hawks. We were crossing the hill on our way to the spot, about a year after photographing the young crows, when I noticed a mass of sticks and rubbish far up a tall oak, which I was quite sure was a crow's nest. I examined it carefully from where I stood and soon caught sight of the tail of the mother, who was sitting in the nest. I rapped on the tree with a stick and was surprised to see a large hawk fly off. We had often seen and heard hawks about the wooded hill when hunting nests and scouting about the "Boxcars"; and I once watched a hawk fly from the large marsh near the west end of the siding with a frog dangling from its claws. We soon found the nest to which it was carrying the frog and were eager to secure pictures of the young hawks.

We returned to the nest in the oak early in June with our cameras, ropes, and a sack for the purpose of securing the pictures and of handling the young hawks as we previously had handled the young crows. We saw that the mother was on the nest as we approached, so stopped and watched her for a few minutes, noticing that a young hawk occasionally stuck its head out from beneath her. The mother flew off eventually and settled in a near-by tree, where she watched us with blazing, defiant eyes.

One of the boys immediately started climbing the tree with one end of the rope tied around his waist. The nest

Young red-shouldered hawks.

was 40 or 50 ft. from the ground and after a long, hard climb he reached it. The young birds were about half grown, pretty downy fellows with sharp eyes, hooked beaks, light, almost snowy heads, and brownish markings about their wings, backs, and tails. We placed them on the branch of a fallen tree and took several pictures of them in a number of poses. They opened their beaks threateningly at first, watched us defiantly, and screamed loudly. However, they soon quieted down and allowed us to handle and work about them without protesting or showing any alarm.

One of the parents returned from a foraging trip while we were busy with the young hawks. It was not at all hard to determine what it had captured for the young to eat. From its claws dangled a large frog. It saw us before

Even the young hawks were large and hawklike
in appearance.

it reached the nest, turned sharply, and hurried off again.

We reached the nest at noon about a week later and at
once saw that the young hawks were still in the nest, so
ate our lunch before attacking the work at hand. Once,
while eating, we heard the adult birds in the distance.
We could see the nest and young hawks from our resting
place and noticed that the latter were now quite large
and were standing up in the nest, watching us. Only once
did one of them move. We noticed that the young hawks
had changed considerable in appearance, also that they
were more hawklike, and had brown markings about

their throats, breasts, and heads. We hid as best we could behind trees after eating our lunch, hoping the parents would visit the nest and feed the young, but this they failed to do. However, we heard them screaming in the distance and saw that they were being chased and bothered by a number of crows. Later, we lowered the youngsters to the ground, in a sack as upon the previous occasion. They now were much harder to handle, fighting, biting, and scratching when the boy tried to put them into the sack. But he was equal to the occasion and soon they were on their way to the ground in the sack elevator, where the anxious photographers were awaiting them.

We perched them in a row upon the branch of a fallen tree, where they stood up and screamed much like their parents. They looked at us defiantly with blazing eyes and wide-open beaks as if ready to bite and scratch at a moment's notice. They now were reddish-brown on the shoulders and gray and brown on the back, wings, and tail. They soon quieted down, however, ceased screaming and threatening us, and posed very nicely for a half-dozen pictures.

I secured two additional glimpses of the young hawks before they left the neighborhood entirely. I visited the wooded hill a few days later and found they still were in the nest. The crows were making fully as much noise in the distance, where they were again waging war upon the parent hawks who were off foraging for their young. One of the parents made a hurried visit to the nest shortly afterwards, remaining but a moment or two and then flying hurriedly off, but not before I had caught a glimpse of its reddish-brown, or chestnut, shoulders.

I found that the young hawks had left the nest when

A boy scout hunting hawks with a camera—the right
way to hunt these useful birds.

I next visited the place, but heard a crow angrily cawing
off toward the southwest, so walked stealthily that way.
There, perched in a tall tree, far from the ground, sat
one of the young hawks. It was carefully watching a crow
that was trying its best to frighten it out of the neighborhood. Finally, the crow darted for the hawk, and the
latter took to its wings and hurriedly flew off. It now was
large and strong of wing and no doubt well able to cope
with crows and other enemies coming its way.

Chapter 9

THE BLUE JAY

" 'THEM blue jays are bad birds, always hanging around our place and bothering the other birds.' My boy put out some wren boxes when he was a little fellow, and we have always had wrens about the place. 'Them is nice little birds.' But a short time ago some blue jays began bothering and trying to drive the wrens away. The boy he wouldn't stand for that. He fixed the pesky things. Now, they stay away!"

Thus spoke a friend in regard to the blue jays, no doubt voicing the feelings of thousands of people. These birds surely have a bad reputation and sometimes suffer cruelly as a consequence. Some folks kill them whenever they get the chance and loudly denounce them whenever one talks to them about birds. Many people, I suspect, would say that my friend's son has the right idea and would loudly applaud his method of dispensing justice to them. For several weeks, one autumn, two blue jays he had "fixed" hung side by side from the top wire of a fence, held securely in place by barbs that had been run into their heads, to serve perhaps as a warning to all other jays.

However, I am wondering if blue jays are half as bad as they are painted; and if there are not far less destructive birds and animals than some people would have us believe. Strictly speaking, there is no such thing as a

A blue jay and thrasher at the bird bath.

bad bird, though a few no doubt are harmful or destructive. On the other hand, many birds do harm on occasion,
a little harm and much good as a general rule, considerable harm and little good rather rarely. Furthermore,
several factors usually must be carefully considered before
one is justified in saying that a given bird is harmful
rather than the reverse.

We have always had blue jays for neighbors and know
of but three instances where they actually have harmed
other birds, the main, if not only, reason for complaint
against them.

A pair of robins built a nest on the pole of a fence near
the house one year, and all went well until the arrival

of the nestlings. Then, one day, a blue jay discovered the nest and pitched the young robins to the ground. We hurried to the rescue and put the robins back into the nest, but a day or two later we found a dead baby robin on the ground beneath the nest. The skin had been torn from its neck, and the body had been mutilated. We strongly suspected the blue jay of killing it, but could not be sure.

Sometime later, a pair of bluebirds had a nest in a box 30 ft. from the house and a pair of jays another in an oak near the garage. In due time, both nests held young birds. One day the mother jay alighted upon the bluebird box, waited until the young birds raised their heads, then thrust her head down the entrance hole, and pulled one out. I heard the alarm notes of the bluebirds, and, upon glancing out, saw the jay on the ground, killing the youngster. Naturally, I shot the jay on the spot. On another occasion I saw a blue jay toss a young kingbird from its nest. I frightened the culprit away, ran for the gun, and returned just in time to shoot it when it returned to the nest a second time.

These are the only jays I ever have killed, and I killed them for the best of reasons. I sometimes wonder if there are not criminals among birds, just as there are robbers and murderers among human beings. However, the fact that there are a few lawless people does not prove that we all are, or that all folks should be executed or imprisoned. Should we not be as fair to the blue jay? The proper procedure of dealing with birds that sometimes do harm, it seems to me, is to punish those actually caught doing harm and to admire, study, and love the rest, blue jays, crows, and blackbirds as well as robins, bluebirds, and meadowlarks.

Young blue jays.

Blue jays, on the other hand, also have their troubles, many of them not being due to their archenemy, man. A pair of these birds nested in the oak grove one year. All went well until the young jays were nearly full grown, when a crow, which had a nest in a near-by woods, began visiting the grove in search of food for her young. Eventually she found the young jays, and, one morning, when I awoke, I heard a great noise about the nest. I soon discovered that the jays were screaming and darting madly at the crow, which was on the ground. I frightened the crow away and found that it had killed a young jay, which it abandoned as I approached. But I hasten to add, in defense of the crow, that this is the only time I have actually known it to kill other birds, and one wanton act does not justify advocating its extermination. Blue jays are among the easiest of birds to attract to the yard by means of food and water; and I always try to have a few of them for neighbors. They visit our bird bath in summer and our food tray in winter; and they come not singly but by twos, threes, and even larger numbers. All birds, as a rule, try to keep other birds at a distance when they are feeding, drinking, or taking a bath, and blue jays are no exception. However, blue jays should not be condemned for this characteristic any more than robins, brown thrashers, chickadees, and bluebirds.

Blue jays nest either in or near the yard each year. Sometimes they successfully raise a brood, sometimes not. It is a well-known fact that a large percentage of the nests built by birds fail to hold the young until they are ready to leave them of their own accord. In other words, there are many tragedies in birdland. But do not the bold blue jays fare better than most birds? No, unless my observations are not correct, they fare no better than most other birds. Apparently, the enemies that are responsible for the loss of many robin, bluebird, and chipping-sparrow nests also take their toll from the jays. When many nests in a given territory are robbed or destroyed, the jays suffer as much as the other birds, indicating that these brightly colored birds are not the culprits.

Two pairs of robins, two pairs of brown thrashers, a pair of blue jays, several pairs of field sparrows, vesper sparrows, a pair of chipping sparrows, bluebirds, flickers, mourning doves, and redheaded woodpeckers nested either in or near the yard one spring and summer. The thrashers built and deserted three nests before they completed the two they used. The robins started no less than six nests and deserted them all before they were half done. It is a curious fact that birds are hard to please early in the season, starting nests they later desert for slight reasons, perhaps after discovering they do not like the locations as well as they thought they were going to. They are harder pressed for time and not so particular as the season advances and then are much more likely to complete and use the nests they start. The first nests started by our robin neighbors were all located in trees, whereas those they completed and used were located on two robin shelves I had built and set out for them.

A pair of blue jays made a determined effort to nest near or in the yard that year. They started the first nest in an oak in the grove; this they never completed for some reason, perhaps because of the visits and depredations of gray squirrels living about the near-by trees. The second nest was built in a young cottonwood a rod from the porch door. This nest was completed and soon held three pretty eggs. Then, one day, I found the robins that were nesting on a shelf on the hen house and the blue jays engaged in bitter warfare. The robins proved the more determined and aggressive, and the jays fled and deserted their nest. Would one be justified in persecuting the robins because they caused the jays to desert their nest? I think not. They were only doing what most birds do in the circumstances, keeping other birds away from what they considered to be their territory. Suppose, on the other hand, the blue jays had been victorious, would one have been justified in persecuting them? The logical and fair answer would be one in the negative. Nevertheless, blue jays, at such times, usually are denounced and either killed or driven away by their human neighbors.

I confess to a strong liking for the blue jay, and this in spite of the fact that I have been obliged to shoot two of them and realize that they sometimes are the enemies of other birds.

A family any bird mother might be proud to claim.

There are many reasons why I like blue jays. In the first place, they are beautiful birds, dressed in neat, black collars, prominent blue crests, and white-tipped tail feathers. In fact, they are among the aristocrats of the bird world. True, in summer, one does not notice them so much, since there then are so many brightly colored birds to be seen, but, in winter, quite the opposite is true.

Secondly, they are permanent residents, to be seen winter and summer alike. Take a walk in winter and the chances are you will see few birds; and the blue jay is quite likely to be among them, perhaps the prettiest and most conspicuous of them all. True, it does not sing, but neither do most of the other winter birds. A blue jay bustling and calling in the winter woods adds color and life. Shouldn't we be thankful for this bit of bright bird life when the cold is numbing and snow and ice are everywhere?

Blue jays also are sociable birds and seem to enjoy the

company of other jays if not of other birds. We find them peaceful and well mannered when they visit our bird bath and food tray, and they are less quarrelsome than some of our other guests. On the whole, they seem to attend to their own affairs pretty well.

These birds are quiet, secretive, and shrewd when nesting, and they love their young and defend their nests with vigor. Only by watching them carefully will you discover the nest, for they are experts at keeping out of sight and never do anything to disclose its whereabouts.

I discovered a jay's nest in a small black oak west of the house one summer and climbed the tree to look at it. Eventually, a blue jay fluttered from the cradle and flew off with loud "jay, jay" notes of alarm. That was the first time I had seen jays either in or near that oak, though the tree stood in plain view of the house and I had passed it dozens of times. The nest held two young jays.

I found another nest in a second oak a rod or two from the tree in which this one was located, two or three years later. This nest held four or five youngsters, of which I decided to take some pictures. The nest was on a branch near the ground, and I used a ladder to reach it. The parents hovered near me as I strapped the camera tripod to the ladder, and, before long one alighted on my hat and perhaps gave it a peck or two.

Blue jays also are many sided, or have many interesting traits or habits, and there is much to be learned in regard to them. And what a variety of call, conversational, and alarm notes they have! These range from their simple "tee, tee, tee," "here, here," and "jay, jay," or "d'jay, d'jay," to their "ge-rul-lup, ge-rul-lup," or is it "de-vel-op, de-vel-op"? Sometimes they utter queer, buzzing notes, and again they imitate the screams of hawks so well that

I surprised this blue jay as she sat on the edge of
the nest looking over her young.

it is hard to detect the difference. Carefully study the
blue jay and see if there is not much to be learned and
admired about it.

Young blue jays, when fully fledged, are pretty, quiet,
and easily handled, and how nicely they pose for pictures.
I once found a jay's nest on a cluster of small branches
springing from the trunk of a swamp oak, about 7 ft.
from the ground. I took a look at it and found that it
held six speckled eggs. When the young jays were nearly
old enough to leave their cradle, I took them from the
nest and photographed them. They were so easily managed that I had little trouble securing all the pictures I
desired before I returned them.

I have taken many pictures of adult jays, some on nests, some at the bird bath, and still others on the food tray. When I set the camera near the bird bath, jays often perch upon it, peck at its bright metal parts, or swing on the string I use for operating the shutter. Often blue jays find their way to the porch in search of food. Since the porch is screened, they sometimes fail to find the hole in the screen by means of which they entered. Then I catch them, pet them a little, after which I set them free.

I found still another blue jay's nest a few days after I found the one in the swamp oak which held four eggs. The mother jay was on this nest and she raised her head slightly and "froze" for concealment. I stood and watched her for some time and saw that she was unusually tame and confiding. Encouraged by this, I decided to try to secure some pictures of her.

I returned to the nest the following morning with the camera, approached it carefully, set the machine 5 ft. from the cradle, and made an exposure. I now made a second with the camera a foot nearer the nest, then a third still closer. I now stood within 2 ft. of the brave bird and thus far not a move had she made. The nest was about 4 ft. from the ground in a thorn tree, in a most excellent position for the taking of pictures.

I now decided to test the bird still further. Slowly, so slowly that it scarcely moved, I extended my hand toward her. Soon the fingers of my extended hand were but 4 in. from her, next three, then two, one, until I touched her. I visited the nest again and again after that, each time taking a picture of her and gently stroking her. I was afraid meanwhile, however, that someone else would find this nest, take advantage of the mother's confiding disposition, and kill her and destroy the nest. All went well, however, and soon the nest held young jays.

I once took a picture of her as she sat on her nest with her back turned toward me and her head raised as usual. I surprised her upon another occasion as she was perched on the rim of the nest looking at her young ones. She raised her head, turned it toward me, then sat perfectly still. I took a picture of her in this position and stroked her without causing her to move. Once, when I was near the nest, she drove a singing meadowlark from the thorn tree, thus showing she was always ready to defend her nest and young from other birds. Only once did she leave her nest while I was near it, when a branch became entangled in the camera and swished near her.

Chapter 10

THE COWBIRD

DOES it not seem strange that some birds are among the worst enemies of other birds? And isn't it surprising that one of the most exquisite of all birds' nests is made by the Baltimore oriole, a member of the same family of birds as the cowbird, which builds no nest but lays its eggs in the nests of other birds? The cowbird is either too lazy or unskillful to build a nest and leaves the incubation of its eggs and the care of its young to the birds it imposes upon.

The cowbird receives its name from its habit of feeding near the feet of grazing cattle, where it finds waste grain, weed seeds, and insects. It is about 7½ in. in length, larger than bluebirds but smaller than robins, or about as large as the Baltimore oriole. The male is mostly black, though about the head, neck, and breast it is a rich coffee brown, whereas the female is grayish-brown, streaked with lighter shades.

The cowbird is a poor singer. Still, his notes are more pleasant than those of grackles and rusty blackbirds. Sometimes one is to be found perched on a telephone pole or wire, or a branch near the top of a tree, raising and spreading his wings, stretching his neck as though nauseated, and uttering notes that sound like "klo-kleece." Some of my friends insist that this sounds like "po-leece," or "po-lice," which it certainly does. The birds imposed

A cowbird at the bird bath.

upon, the song, vesper, lark, chipping, and field sparrows, the wood thrush, bluebird, catbird, phoebe, and warblers, however, should be calling "po-lice" and not the cowbird.

Cowbirds undoubtedly do considerable harm to the birds they impose upon, although I doubt if this is as great as some writers would have us believe. Each mother lays many eggs, variously estimated at from four or five to a dozen or more in a season, often in the nests of smaller birds. The cowbirds' eggs sometimes hatch before those of the owners, and the young cowbirds have great appetites, secure more than their share of food perhaps, grow rapidly, and sometimes squirm and crowd the rightful eggs or young from the nest. The rightful eggs thus treated are lost, broken, or fail to hatch, while the young usually perish from exposure and starvation.

Full to the brim. This nest held five song sparrow's
and two cowbird's eggs.

I once made a study of the activities of cowbirds, finding many nests of other birds in which they deposited
their eggs. I found a phoebe's nest on a ledge inside a
boxcar early in May, that held one phoebe's egg and a
cowbird's egg; this nest held four phoebe's eggs and the
cowbird's egg on the ninth. The cowbird's egg had
hatched by the twentieth, but the phoebe's eggs had not.
The young cowbird was quite large by the end of the
month and seemed to have little enough room in the
nest; a small dead phoebe lay on the boxcar floor, where
it had been kicked or crowded by the young cowbird;
and one phoebe's egg lay beneath the interloper, while
two others were missing. The last phoebe's egg failed to
hatch, though the young cowbird got safely away. Four
phoebes were lost to bring one young cowbird to maturity
in this instance.

A song sparrow's nest was found a short distance off

The nest of a yellow warbler containing a cowbird's egg.

that held three sparrow's and two cowbird's eggs. Here at least one of the sparrow's eggs hatched before the second young cowbird was out of the shell. All of the young birds were lost when this nest was destroyed by a cat or some other night prowler. A yellow warbler's nest also was located near by, which held a warbler's egg and two cowbird's eggs. The cowbird's eggs were removed from this nest — to save the young warbler when it arrived, if such a thing were possible. This nest was found empty and deserted a few days later, in spite of the fact that a twig was used in removing the cowbird's eggs. No doubt this nest was doomed from the start. Still, it is not the easiest thing in the world for a person to interfere and save our pretty songsters from cowbirds.

I found the nest of a lark sparrow about the middle of July that held three cowbird's and two sparrow's eggs.

It held a young sparrow and two young cowbirds when I next visited it. A hollow stump a few rods distant contained a bluebird's nest that held three cowbird's eggs and one bluebird's egg. Here were two nests only a few rods apart that held six of the eggs of this shirker. Cowbirds must have been numerous in that neighborhood and must have had little trouble finding the cradles of other birds, whether these were located within hollow stumps or hidden in the grass on the ground.

Many nests of small birds that have been imposed upon are found to be full to the brim with eggs, since they were built to accommodate the eggs of the owners only. Imagine what a situation is created when cowbirds lay two or three eggs in such nests. Many of the eggs, no doubt, fail to hatch because they cannot be kept warm. The little birds do their best to heat and incubate all the eggs, but usually are unable to do so.

I ran across an old yellow warbler's nest, in a bush early in the spring, which seemed unusually deep. Apparently it was a two-story affair. I removed the top section and found an egg buried beneath it; the egg proved to be that of a cowbird, which the outraged owners had successfully gotten rid of when they discovered it was not their own. I found a similar nest, which, upon examination, proved to be a three-story affair, in which two cowbird's eggs had been buried. Thus does the little yellow warbler outwit the cowbird. Instances are on record where yellow warblers have built four-story nests, in which they have buried three or more cowbird's eggs, one or more at a time.

Two song sparrows' nests were found later that same spring that held two cowbird's eggs each. One of these nests held three sparrow's eggs, the other five. The nest

The nest of a vesper sparrow containing a cowbird's egg.

with five sparrow's eggs and two cowbird's eggs seemed to be overflowing, since it was a very shallow affair. I removed the cowbirds' eggs from both nests, but never learned what effect this had.

A new yellow warbler's nest was located in June, and from it I removed a cowbird's egg. It held four warbler's eggs and another cowbird's egg a few days later; I removed the latter also. Four other yellow warblers' nests were found about the same time, all of which held cowbird's eggs. I found one of the four overturned and the eggs it held on the ground, when I visited them a few days later and removed the cowbirds' eggs from the remaining three. I next visited these nests later in the month and was pleased to find that all were still safe

The nest of a wood thrush containing cowbird's eggs.

and that all held young warblers. I had, indeed, succeeded in saving four pairs of these pretty and useful
birds from the impositions of cowbirds and had perhaps
saved sixteen young warblers from miserable deaths by
exposure or starvation.

I secured two additional glimpses of the activities of
cowbirds before the month of June was up, hearing the
sharp notes of alarm of a pair of song sparrows on the
first of these occasions. I stopped, watched, and listened,
hoping to discover the whereabouts of a nest. I waited
for a long time, but the parent birds gave me no clue
as to what they were guarding, so started to leave, frightening a young cowbird from the grass as I did so. The

A field sparrow's nest deserted by its owners after
cowbirds had laid two eggs in it.

song sparrows at once flew to the young cowbird, hovered
solicitously near it, chirped anxiously, and seemed more
alarmed than ever. Here, then, was the reason for their
alarm and anxiety. They had reared a young cowbird
and were still feeding and guarding it though it was
fully fledged and considerably larger than its foster parents. I searched for some time, hoping to find at least
one young sparrow hiding in the grass, but without success, so concluded, as often is the case, that the young
sparrows had long since perished and that the young
cowbird was the sole survivor.

Cowbirds are especially active during the months of
May, June, and July, the height of the breeding season.
At this time the females are often to be seen sneaking
about woods and fields and inspecting trees, vines, bushes,
and suitable places on the ground for nests in which to
deposit their eggs. I caught sight of one just before the
end of June that seemed to realize she was about wicked

business and that acted as though she had been caught in the very act of violating another bird's nest. She stretched her neck to watch me and tried her best to hide behind some leaves to avoid being seen.

I have spent considerable time the past twenty years hunting for the nests of birds and have found hundreds of them built by scores of species. Many of these nests contained the eggs of cowbirds, particularly those of field, chipping, lark, song, and vesper sparrows, wood and Wilson's thrushes, redstarts, Maryland yellowthroats, and yellow warblers, less often those of catbirds, brown thrashers, red-winged blackbirds, and meadowlarks. As a matter of fact, a comparatively large percentage of the nests of warblers and sparrows contain the eggs of cowbirds.

Most birds seem to be helpless when imposed upon by cowbirds; indeed, many do not even seem to realize they have been imposed upon, singing and going about their affairs as if nothing were wrong. The eggs of field, song, and vesper sparrows, though smaller, look somewhat like those of cowbirds, so the fact that these birds frequently are fooled is not so hard to understand. Or aren't they fooled and only make the best of a bad matter? The eggs of warblers differ more, while those of bluebirds, catbirds, veeries, wood thrushes, phoebes, and red-winged blackbirds are quite unlike those of cowbirds, so these birds should at once discover the imposition. The only birds that seem capable of outwitting the cowbird are field and chipping sparrows, the catbird, brown thrasher, and yellow warbler. Many birds, no doubt, desert their nests if cowbirds lay eggs in them. I frequently find the nests of field and chipping sparrows near the house that hold cowbirds' eggs but no sparrows' eggs, subsequent

The eggs of a cowbird in the nest of a brown thrasher.

observations proving they have been deserted. However, I doubt if these birds desert their nests if they hold both rightful and cowbirds' eggs. Yellow warblers outwit cowbirds by building additions to their cradles, but, though they are willing to bury the eggs of cowbirds, it is a question if they do so when their own eggs also must be sacrificed.

I learned how one of the smartest of our birds successfully coped with the cowbird a few years ago. I was crossing a sandy, rolling hill dotted with many stately black oaks, when I discovered a brown thrasher's nest on the ground that held three thrasher's eggs and two cowbird's eggs. I was able to keep a close watch over this nest because it was about 80 rods from the house. The next time

Three hungry young cowbirds.

I visited the place I found that the thrashers had either removed or destroyed the cowbirds' eggs. The mother was on the nest when I arrived and, beneath her, lay only her own eggs. Not a trace of the cowbird's was to be found. That is exactly how one would expect a shrewd, sensitive, alert bird like the brown thrasher to handle such a situation.

Only once have I caught a cowbird in the very act of laying an egg in another bird's nest. I found this bird sitting in a chipping sparrow's nest in a grapevine clinging to our west porch; the details of this imposition will be given more fully in a later chapter devoted to the friendly and confiding "chippy."

Though much can be said to the detriment of the cowbird, something also can be said in its favor. To be sure, it lays it eggs in the nests of other birds, causes the owners much extra work and anxiety, and is responsible for the loss of many young birds. On the other hand, it does some good, eating many weed seeds and destroying some

insects. In fact, there is nothing to be noticed about its
feeding habits that indicates it is not fully as useful as
many other birds with much better reputations. Cowbirds frequently feed near me in the garden and field,
where they catch and destroy many pests, often following
the plow and eating the cutworms and other pests uncovered. At such times they prove tame and confiding,
alighting upon the ground near the feet of the horses,
walking briskly to and fro, and patiently waiting and
hunting insects for hours. And the person interested in
the songs of birds finds something of interest and a little
music in the notes of the cowbird.

Nor was every cowbird to be seen reared at the expense
of four or five pretty and useful birds, nor should it as a
species be exterminated. A few of them are worth having,
if for no other reason than that they are not like other
birds. If they get too numerous, ways and means for
keeping them in check will no doubt be found; meanwhile who is bold enough to assert that the balance of
nature should be disturbed by their wholesale destruc-
tion? If they are numerous in your neighborhood, and
if they lay their eggs in the nests of your desirable bird
neighbors, remove the runt eggs with twigs, otherwise
little needs be done.

I spent no little time one summer watching a field
sparrow's nest that held two sparrow's eggs and two
cowbird's eggs. I watched it very carefully after the eggs
hatched, for fear the young cowbirds would crowd the
young sparrows from the nest or would secure the bulk
of the food brought by the parents, but nothing happened
to warrant any interference on my part. I placed an umbrella blind near this nest and watched the adult sparrows
feeding the young birds. They often fitted a caterpillar,

katydid, butterfly, or moth to several mouths before finding a youngster hungry enough to swallow the tidbit at a gulp. The young birds, so far as I could determine, were fed pretty much in turn; and, best of all, the young sparrows, as well as the young cowbirds, were successfully reared.

Chapter 11

THE MEADOWLARK

WHAT a musical, useful, and neighborly bird the meadowlark is. It is a winter bird in many parts of our country, but in the northern tier of states it is seldom to be seen during the months of December, January, and February. Sometimes, late in February, I see and hear a meadowlark, but you may be sure that it is only in those years when there is little snow and the weather mild. It usually does not return to our neighborhood much before the middle of March.

The meadowlark is to be seen and heard about fields and meadows, where the grass is tall and dense. It nervously spreads and twitches its tail when you get near it and utters notes of alarm that sound like the word *still* repeated over and over and sometimes drawn out into a series of "ll-ll-l" notes. "Still, still, still-ll-ll-l" is exactly what it sometimes seems to say. It also has another note one frequently hears, no doubt an alarm note, that may be written "zeet." Off it flies when you get too near it, first flapping its wings vigorously and then holding them spread and motionless, but after a comparatively short flight drops into the grass again in the distance, where it hides and looks about until it is sure no lurking enemies are near.

The song of the meadowlark is one of the most pleasant of all birds' songs. It is not varied, nor bubbling, nor

A meadowlark with a cutworm.

long continued, but possesses much charm nevertheless, a loud, sweet, clear, whistled "spring-o'-the-year," uttered while the bird is conspicuously perched on a post, telephone pole, or the branch of a tree. The meadowlark also frequently sings when flying, and even while on the ground, especially when near or accompanied by its mate. Sometimes the singing birds seem to say: "Spring is here; spring is here," or "Spring, spring is here," or "Spring, lovely spring." And at other times, when the nesting season is well advanced, the songs of these birds may be written thus: "Tee-del-dee-dee-del-dee." Often a number of meadowlarks are to be heard singing at the same time from various parts of the same field or meadow, and then the air is filled with whistled music that always makes the bird lover feel in the best of spirits.

Meadowlarks usually migrate in small, loose, scattered flocks, coming as it were in small waves, all the males in full song. Many of them pass on to points farther north, though a few drop out and make their summer home with us. These birds migrate in much the same way in autumn, when the days are cool and frosty, and the males are fully as musical. Indeed, many, bright, frosty autumn days remind one of the first springlike days of March, since then the meadowlarks sing in much the same way and fully as freely, as if the seasons had in some way become reversed and it once again were spring.

The meadowlark builds a snug nest of grass on the ground, carefully hiding it in a tuft of dry grass or beneath the leaves of a dandelion or other large plant. Tunnels or paths often lead through the grass to the cradles, some of which are attractive dome-shaped affairs with circular holes in their sides. From four to six white eggs speckled with brown are laid in each nest. The mother remains quietly in her nest when there are intruders about and relies upon the protective colors of her plumage for concealment. Many meadowlarks avoid being discovered by thus hiding and generally succeed in keeping the locations of their nests a secret. Get too near a nest, however, and off she flutters, returning after you are safely off in the distance.

The meadowlark is chubby of build and becomingly dressed, its yellow breast being marked with a conspicuous dark crescent which shows to splendid advantage when the bird is seen from the front. It has a habit of turning its back toward the observer, perhaps so as not to attract too much attention, apparently realizing that this is streaked with black, brown, and gray and thus inconspicuous. Its outer tail feathers are white and usually show up well when the bird is alarmed or excited and spreading its tail, and also when it is flying from the observer.

Insects constitute 74 per cent of the meadowlark's food supply (grasshoppers, crickets, ground beetles, and cater-

The nest and eggs of a meadowlark.

pillars mainly) and weed seeds and waste grain most of the rest. Cutworms are taken in large numbers in April, May, and June, when they are most numerous, and grasshoppers later in the summer.

We have long had meadowlarks for near neighbors during the nesting season, and many of them have nested about the premises, sometimes in old fields, sometimes in the orchard, and again near the oak grove. A pair nested less than 3 rods from the house one year, in some tall grass between the yard and grove. March the twelfth was meadowlark day, for on that date I heard and saw the first one of the season. It had been raining lightly for a day or two, and, the evening of the eleventh, we were sure the wind was going to shift to the northwest and that the usual cold snap would follow. Instead, we found to our pleasure and surprise in the morning that the wind was blowing from the southwest and that it actually was balmy. I heard the familiar notes of blackbirds when I first stepped outside and soon saw a flock — no doubt a mixed flock of red-wings and grackles — then heard the sweet whistled "spring-o'-the-year" of a meadowlark. The children and I walked as far as the end of the pasture, where we found him perched near the top of a large black oak; he flew off as we approached, but sang his delightful song as he did so.

Meadowlarks were to be seen and heard daily from then on, and sometimes small bands of them enlivened the neighboring fields, meadows, and pastures with their clear songs. A more delightful place than a field or pasture frequented by a number of singing meadowlarks is hard to imagine. Two or more of them spent considerable time either in or near the yard as the weeks passed and the weather became warmer, and I once caught sight of two males sparring near the house, both being very quick and aggressive. The bird that was attacked took no chances of being injured by his rival's fierce darts and wisely dodged a few times and then hurriedly left. It was one of these same birds, no doubt, that was singing cheerfully near the house a few days later, when along came a second and alighted near it. The second had heard the first, had recognized it as a rival, and had decided to find and drive it out of the neighborhood at all costs, since he came all ruffled up as if very angry and ready for instant hostilities. The first bird was not in a fighting mood, however, at once hurrying off without stopping to make a single protest. Soon a pair of the birds frequented the grassy plot of ground

A young meadowlark hiding in the tall grass.

north of the house, where they apparently intended to nest.

The male now sang daily from the near-by trees, posts, and bushes, or uttered his warning "still-still-still-ll-ll-l" when we visited the vicinity. I often hunted for the nest, but did not find it until the middle of May, when I systematically searched for it, finding it 3 rods from the house in a tuft of dry grass. Out darted the mother from the cunningly concealed cradle, which had a low, arched entrance and held four eggs.

The eggs hatched a few days later, and, early in June, I placed an umbrella blind near the nest to learn more about our neighbors. I remained inside the blind for an hour on June second, but saw neither of the owners near the nest meanwhile, although I did hear their alarm notes and occasionally caught sight of them in the distance.

I entered the blind at 9:45 on June third, and, five minutes later, the mother was to be seen making her way

toward the nest. She walked briskly along, crouched as
much as possible, so as to keep out of sight, and
meandered through the grass as she carefully selected
the best path. Occasionally she stopped, stretched to her
full height, glanced rather furtively to the right and left,
and then looked long and intently at the blind. Sometimes, when the wind shook the tent, she quickly retraced
her steps a short distance, but finally reached the nest,
where she remained for about a minute with her little
ones, sitting just in front of the entrance and facing them.
The young birds chirped loudly as they begged for the
food she brought. She was back with additional food at
10:14, this time with a large mouthful. She proved herself an excellent housekeeper, for she carefully cleaned
the nest. She was back with a spider with a large egg
sac about a minute later. No sooner had she given this
to a youngster than a gust of wind shook the blind
violently, frightening her off a few steps, where she found
a cutworm which she fed her young.

I spent two hours within the blind on June third and
another on the fourth, and, during this time, the mother
fed the young seventeen times, seven times offering them
great mouthfuls of mangled pests. Once, though she
had a very large mouthful, I noticed she had a cutworm;
twice she had three of these pests; and, all told, she fed
the young at least eleven of them. Many of the cutworms
were alive and performed all sorts of twists and turns
with the free parts of their bodies in their efforts to get
away. Meadowlarks destroy large numbers of cutworms
during the months of May and June, if not in April and
July also. Cutworms are among the worst of farm and
garden pests and destroy large numbers of corn, melon,
cabbage, tomato, and other plants. Most birds feed their

young from daylight till dark, so I estimated that our meadowlarks destroyed sixty cutworms during their fifteen- or sixteen-hour day, for a grand total of six hundred in ten days.

My attention was mainly centered upon the mother and what she was feeding her young. Nevertheless, I noticed that the youngsters were quite large and that they moved about a good deal in the nest, yawning, stretching, flapping their wings, preening, and sometimes chirping. The male made no effort to feed the young, leaving that entirely to his mate, but he sang a great deal and faithfully remained on guard. I noticed that when he sang she seemed less frightened than at other times. Sometimes, while working her way toward the nest with food, she edged this way and that, hesitated, and retreated until she heard his lovely whistled song; then her whole attitude changed and she made her way to the cradle with little fussing.

Chapter 12

THE BALTIMORE ORIOLE

IT IS early May when I hear this talkative bird for the first time, after which it is a neighbor for several weeks, since many of them nest about the house. The Baltimore oriole is our most common oriole and is found as far north as Canada in summer; it winters in Central America, Mexico, and northern South America.

I nearly always hear this bird before I see it, for it returns to its breeding grounds with a song in its heart. What a strong, healthy voice it has and what strange things it sometimes seems to say when singing! "Eat it, Potter, eat it" is how Thoreau interpreted its notes; "ta ra-ra, boom, de-aye" someone else has written it; and "Will you really? Truly?," "Coming over to see you," "Here, here, here, pretty," and "Potatoes, plant right here" the present writer has written it at various times the past twenty years.

What the first orioles to return seem to say when singing, the later arrivals also say; and sometimes the same song is to be heard for several years. One year in four or five, however, is likely to be a surprise year because the oriole returns with a new song. The year 1938 proved such a year, for this bird returned with a most delightful, new song, singing "Hear, hear, hear sweet music!" Nor need you be in doubt as to the identity of the author,

A male Baltimore oriole enjoying a bath.

for the oriole has a rich alto voice that is quite unlike that of most birds.

The male is a gorgeous fellow dressed in orange, black, and white, being black about the head, neck, throat and upper back, orange on the rump and underneath, orange and black about the tail, and orange, black, and white about the wings. Fire bird, golden oriole, and golden robin he also is called.

Baltimore orioles have at various times nested in the oaks about the barnyard, in trees in the pasture and grove, and in a bur oak standing 6 ft. from the corner of the house, though not with as great regularity as in a tall oak located a little farther away. I usually can count upon orioles nesting near the top of the latter each year, perhaps because they have long used it and hence have a strong liking for it. Perhaps the orioles now nesting there were reared in a pouched nest near its top; what, then,

The nest of the Baltimore oriole.

can be more natural than that they should wish to raise their own young amid its friendly branches?

Last summer, as usual, these birds used it, building their cradle near the tip of a branch on the southeast side, some 40 or 50 ft. from the ground. The mother is the architect, weaving one of the finest and best of all birds' nests and securely fastening it to leaves and twigs. I happened to be sitting in the grove one evening late in May, when I noticed a rustling of the leaves near the tip of the branch. There she was, hard at work and intensely interested, paying no attention to the fact that there was a human being near, watching her. Orioles build so far from the ground that they are little concerned with what is taking place on the earth beneath them. Were one to get on the same level with them in some way, for instance by climbing the tree, things would be different, I suspect, and they might scold, sputter, complain, and perhaps desert the place as some other birds do under similar circumstances. Naturally, a nest thus located, made, and securely anchored is about as safe a place as can be imagined in which young birds may be reared.

The nests are hard to see when in use, as they usually are hidden by leaves; then, too, they are far from the ground so that one is obliged to look against the light, which is not easy. Consequently, I do not find some of the nests my oriole neighbors build until autumn, when the trees are bare.

Sometimes, toward spring, we find an old oriole's nest on the ground. I happen to have such a fallen nest before me, which we found beneath the favorite oak, a snug, stout basket, not as deep and pouched as some to be found, but a most substantial structure nevertheless. Ten leaves had been partly woven into it. It was anchored to these no doubt, and, when they fell, the cradle fell also. Had the nest been anchored to twigs instead of leaves, it would have hung there for years, for I was obliged to exert considerable force when removing the leaves from the structure, even when I took them one by one. The main part of the nest was made of plant down, plant fibers, an occasional thread or piece of string, and was lined with fine grass, having a uniform light-gray color on the outside. The eggs are white, and usually number from four to six in a nest. They are scrawled with black or dark brown and resemble those of red-winged blackbirds.

It sometimes is possible to stand near or beneath trees holding nests and watch the parents feeding the young. The young birds screech, squirm, jostle each other about, and make considerable noise as they beg for food, the din and action increasing as they grow older. Then the nests are easily located, since all one needs to do is listen.

Orioles are birds of the treetops. That is where you usually will find the young after they desert the nest, accompanied, of course, by their parents, the family parties roaming wherever their appetites and fancies lead them. The young have characteristic, immature oriole voices and plaintive notes, and, once these are known, the birds easily may be located by means of them. Young and adult birds frequently descend to the ground for a drink and bath when thirsty and warm, then return to their leafy, treetop retreat.

Orioles are useful birds, 84 per cent of their food consisting of animal matter (insects mainly) according to studies made by the United States Department of Agriculture. Caterpillars are eaten freely and constitute 34 per cent of the total food. They also destroy many beetles, bugs, ants, grasshoppers, and some wasps and spiders. "The beetles are principally click beetles, the larvae of which are among the most destructive insects known; and the bugs include plant and bark lice, both very harmful, but so small and obscure as to be passed over unnoticed by most birds. Ants are eaten mostly in spring, grasshoppers in July and August, and wasps and spiders with considerable regularity throughout the season."

The vegetable matter amounts to 16 per cent. This pretty bird sometimes does some harm in the garden, where it takes a few berries and many green peas. The birds split the pods of the latter, eat the peas, and leave only empty husks behind.

Chapter 13

THE RED-WINGED BLACKBIRD

YOU must take a walk to some near-by marsh, pond, or stream, if you wish to see and make the acquaintance of the red-winged blackbird, a common, musical, and likable bird that makes its home among the cattails, reeds, marsh grasses, and willows. During the spring and early summer you are quite sure to hear the pleasant songs of the males, who perch on the tops of tall cattails, willows, and other objects, where they are conspicuous and sometimes can be seen for a long distance when thus engaged.

The red-winged blackbird arrives from its winter home in the southern part of the United States early in the spring, generally about the second week in March. Some bright mild morning, when you first step outside, you hear its "tchack" call and catch sight of one or more of them flying by overhead, bound for some stream or pond, though one or more may drop to the top of a tree and sing for you. After you have heard and seen your first bluebird or robin, you should be on the lookout for this bird, since it migrates at about the same time; and, like the bluebird and robin, it remains with us until late in the autumn, sometimes as late as the latter part of November.

The red-wing is almost as large as the robin, the former being 9½ in. in length, the latter 10, so if we

Three young red-winged blackbirds.

think of the two as being of about the same size that is close enough for all practical purposes. As the name indicates, it is a black bird which has bright patches of red and yellow on its wings, and these bright epaulets or wing patches are the field marks by means of which it may at once be known.

Have you heard the blackbird chorus or choir in the spring and autumn, that great convention of red-wings and their cousins, that marks the gathering of the clans at about migration time? This choir is worth going a distance to hear. True, the birds are noisy and all of them chatter and gabble at the same time, but it is a regular part of their lives. After singing and chattering in unison for a long time, they move on to some other tree, or descend to the ground for lunch, marching up and down in companies and regiments and devouring waste grain, weed seeds, and perhaps insects.

The red-wing nests among cattails, reeds, marsh grasses, and willows of swamps and marshes, though

most any watery spot overgrown with some kind of vegetation is likely to furnish a pair of them with a summer
home. The nest is made of muck and marsh grass and
perhaps a few cattail leaves; it is cup-shaped and fastened
securely to cattails, willows, and other tall plants. Each
nest holds from three to five bluish-white eggs that are
boldly scrawled with black. "The eggs looked as though
they were cracked" one of my boy-scout friends said when
describing the eggs of the red-wing, and, when he said
that, I knew he had actually found a nest and carefully
examined the eggs it contained.

The red-winged blackbird's song is one of the most
pleasant of all spring sounds, a musical "chonk-er-ee," or
"konk-er-ee," that has a flutelike quality, or is it, as some
of my scout friends insist, "straw-ber-ries"? If you do not
like these, you have Emerson's famous interpretation of
"o-ka-lee," which sometimes fits this bird's song to per-
fection. It raises its wings when it sings, and in this habit
resembles its relatives, the cowbird, grackle, rusty blackbird, and yellow-headed blackbird. It has a number of
call and alarm notes, also, which you are sure to hear if
you pay it a visit during the nesting season.

As a rule, several pairs of red-wings are to be found
nesting in the same place, usually in a marsh well overgrown with cattails, perhaps where they have marsh
wrens, yellow-headed blackbirds, and swamp sparrows
for neighbors; and each nest seems to be a community
affair. If you get near a nest, the owners cry out and all
the other blackbirds within hearing come to the rescue.
How they scold, sputter, and chatter! And the nearer you
get to the nest, the more noise they make and the nearer
they come to you, sometimes fluttering and crying with
flapping wings just above you.

A nest was built in this perilous place.

You will hardly recognize the mother birds, for they look quite unlike the more handsome males, being smaller, dingy birds with streaked suits. However, if you see one leaving a cup-shaped nest securely fastened to a cattail in a marshy place, you should at once guess you are looking at a mother red-wing.

Although more than 50 per cent of the red-wing's food consists of weed seeds, according to studies made by the United States Department of Agriculture, this handsome bird sometimes proves a pest. This is especially true in the upper Mississippi Valley, where the birds congregate in great flocks after the nesting season. These great flocks no doubt roost about the marshes and sloughs bordering the great river, but travel inland for no little distance during the day to feed, and one of the familiar sights of the valley is to see streams of these birds flying inland in the morning, but riverwards in the late afternoon, the

The nest and eggs of a red-winged blackbird.

birds appearing in companies, or long ribbonlike streams, taking almost the same route, and flying by for an hour or more, thousands upon thousands of them.

These great flocks visit cornfields when the grain is in the milk, tear the husk apart at the tip of the ear, and feast upon the delicious kernels. The corn thus treated becomes infested with insects, spoils perhaps, and sometimes fails to ripen properly. A large flock can ruin a field of the grain in a short time, so the farmers are obliged to remain on guard during this critical time, shotgun in hand, ready to wage war upon the birds.

The population of the United States is constantly increasing, and as it increases has a tendency to rob many birds of nesting places. True, many birds like the house wren, robin, and purple martin, which find city life congenial, are not greatly affected, but others that shun civilization have a harder time. As they are being driven farther and farther off, they are finding it harder and harder to secure suitable nesting places, and are decreasing in numbers.

This encroachment upon the birds' domain is especially great about our large cities, where all the underbrush is destroyed whenever a new building is erected, where every marsh, that place so dear to many birds, is filled or drained, thus depriving them of nesting places. The observations I made of a pair of nesting red-wings one spring shows to what lengths many birds are now forced to go to rear a brood and how we are robbing many of nesting places.

Among the first birds to arrive from their southern winter home that year were the red-winged blackbirds. I was surprised to hear their "chonk-er-ees" coming from the dead, brown cattails of a little marsh to the rear of a great steel plant near the center of a busy manufacturing city. This little marsh was triangular in shape, bounded by two railway embankments and a dumping place, and was rapidly being filled with brick, sand, gravel, cinders, and other waste materials from the mill, which stood about 100 ft. away.

I saw the red-wings hovering about this little triangular marsh for several weeks and was always greeted by the merry "chonk-er-ee" of the male whenever I passed the place. I was quite sure the birds were either nesting or thinking of nesting there and usually stopped long enough to give the reeds and marsh grasses a casual inspection in hopes of discovering the cradle.

I heard the alarm notes of the male as I approached one

A nest with young red-winged blackbirds.

morning after a few days' absence and soon saw the female emerge from the cattails, uttering anxious notes as she did so. I decided to find the nest this time if possible, so walked slowly about the marsh, parting the reeds and marsh grasses next the shore, but failed to find it. I next secured two small planks from the dump; by means of these I worked my way across one end of the marsh, where the cattails and marsh grass were thickest. I stepped from one plank to the other, moving the one I had just used ahead of the other, and thus managed to keep from sinking too deeply into the soft, muddy bottom. I got safely across at last, though not without many misgivings concerning my unsteady and slowly sinking planks, but again failed to find the nest. Once across and again upon solid ground, I carefully examined the opposite edge of the marsh, not overlooking a single cattail, and finally found it directly across from where I stood. I had stood near the nest when I first circled the marsh, so near I could have touched it with my foot, but had failed to find it because my attention was centered on the vegetation at the center of the pond and not on that near the shore. I should have realized the nest was near me, for all the time I stood there the male bird fluttered just above my head and uttered his shrill notes of alarm.

The nest was fastened to two clusters of cattails and was about 1 ft. above the water; waste materials from the mill were being dumped about it and were breaking down and burying cattails within 3 ft. of it. I circled the marsh to look at it, and the male again became greatly alarmed and fluttered and cried above me. The nest held two eggs and a young bird just out of the shell.

I hurriedly took two pictures of it and was about to leave when a workman brought a load of waste materials for the dump. Naturally, he looked at me in a surprised way, for he was not expecting to find anyone there. I pointed to the cradle, and asked him if he knew it were there. He replied that he had not seen it before, but that he had often wondered why the birds seemed so alarmed when he arrived with his loads. He became greatly interested in the little bird home and told me of many experiences he had had with birds in Europe, but especially about one he called the "cuckoo bird," whose eggs he had often found in the nests of other birds. The bird he referred to was the European cuckoo, which has habits similar to our cowbird, which never builds a nest but slyly deposits its eggs in the cradles of other birds.

I was pleased to find this workman interested in the birds and thanked him for his assurance that the nest would not be destroyed. I found him as good as his word, for he told the other workmen about the nest and asked them to dump their loads some distance from the cradle. Later I again visited this unsightly little marsh and found the nest still safe and sound and the last of the young birds about to leave it.

Chapter 14

THE VESPER SPARROW

MOST bird students have favorites — birds that have endeared themselves to them in various ways: by their songs, unobtrusive ways, charming dress, confiding character, and neighborly habits. One of my favorites is the vesper sparrow, which is a sweet singer, always much in evidence but never bold, noisy, or troublesome, highly useful, and has always been a near neighbor of ours.

One often hears a lovely bird song coming from across the fields during the morning and evening hours early in April. The song consists of runs and trills, interspersed with "chees" and whistled notes, the first ones being louder and uttered more slowly than the latter. This is the song of the vesper sparrow, which is hard to describe but of such a nature it at once enables you to identify its author correctly, provided you have previously heard it and have it well in mind.

Take a walk in the direction from which the notes seem to come and you usually will have little trouble discovering the songster. Were someone to point it out to you, you would at once say it is a sparrow of some kind, for it is dressed in a typical sparrow's suit of gray and brown. As likely as not, you find it perched on the top of a post, a tall weed, or near the end of a lower branch of a tree. Watch it carefully and notice that it raises its head as it sings its inspiring song, the mandibles moving

A vesper sparrow at the bird bath.

rapidly and the throat pulsating as the notes are uttered. The song over, the bird lowers its head, looks about, preens its feathers, and then sings again.

But aside from its song, how does one know the bird is a vesper sparrow? In the first place, its throat, breast, and sides are streaked. Secondly, by looking at it closely with a field glass, we find that its shoulders are reddish, which has given it the name bay-winged bunting. More important, it has white outer tail feathers — the field mark of identification.

There is but one other sparrow that has white along the sides of the tail — the lark sparrow — with which the vesper sparrow is likely to be confused. However, the lark sparrow has several white-tipped tail feathers just inside the outer ones, and its tail, when spread, as it frequently is when the bird is alarmed, courting, or flying, looks like a tiny fan with a pretty white border. It also has a brown crown, brown patches over the ears, a spot in the center of the breast, and dark lines through the eyes and along the lower edges of the cheeks.

While a singing vesper sparrow is often to be found perched on the top of a post or tall weed, this bird is a typical ground bird. It lives largely upon weed seeds and insects it secures from the ground; it loves to take dust baths in roads, gardens, and fields; and it always nests on the ground. Take a walk through a field or treeless pasture, or drive along a dusty country road, where vesper sparrows are numerous, and the birds will dart from the ground, flit from weed to weed, or post to post, ahead of you, showing their white outer tail feathers during each brief stage of their forward progress.

The vesper, or bay-winged, sparrow is our true field sparrow, though another (*Spizella pusilla*) is known by that name. The field sparrow does not nest in fields but in brushy pastures and about the borders of woods, in clusters of weeds and grasses, in bushes, and other similar places, while the vesper sparrow always builds on the ground, sometimes in slight depressions, but more often beside weeds, in tufts of grass, piles of leaves and rubbish, and in hills of beans, corn, and potatoes. Some nests are built on spots so free from vegetation that there is not a weed or blade of grass to mark their locations. Burroughs very appropriately calls the vesper sparrow the field sparrow or grass finch, and the field sparrow the wood or bush sparrow. The nest is made of tiny weeds, fine grass, and hair, and the eggs are white but rather evenly speckled with darker shades.

The incubating or brooding mother remains in the nest until you are right beside it, then flushes, spreads her tail, drags her wings, and utters sharp notes of alarm.

The umbrella blind at the nest of a vesper sparrow
marked by a stake to the right.

Off she goes, trying her best to make you think she has
been injured and doing all she can to attract your attention and keep you from finding the cradle.

Have you heard the vesper sparrow's evensong?
Although this bird sings sweetly throughout the day, it
also sings long and sweetly late in the day, often after 8
o'clock at night in June, when most other birds are
silent. If you have not heard this song, listen for it. It may
be soft and low, because it comes from across the fields;
and it has a drowsy, peaceful quality. It is, in fact, a
sweet pastoral hymn. Is it any wonder, then, that this
charming and useful songster is known far and wide
as the vesper sparrow?

The nest and eggs of a vesper sparrow.

But in spite of its valuable feeding habits and sweet song, the vesper sparrow has a hard time rearing a brood, this being due to its choice of a nesting place. Many nests are destroyed by livestock, machinery, and vehicles; others are robbed by snakes, skunks, and other animals; and still others have the eggs of cowbirds deposited in them. I usually find a dozen or more vesper sparrow's nests each year, few of which have not previously been found and used by cowbirds, some holding but one cowbird's egg, others two or more. One that I found in the garden directly behind the house one year held one sparrow's egg and three cowbird's eggs. The latter all hatched but the former did not, and the poor deluded sparrows worked early and late to supply the young cowbirds with food. I perched the young pot-bellied interlopers in a row

A vesper sparrow brooding.

on a branch when they were nearly large enough to leave the nest and took their pictures, then returned them to their cradle. They proved tractable enough and posed very nicely with wide-open, hungry mouths.

In spite of the cowbirds and many tragedies and other hardships, the vesper sparrows always seem in the best of spirits. If their nests are destroyed, they at once build others to take their places, and, if these are violated by cowbirds, they do their best to incubate all the eggs and solicitously care for both their own and their foster children. No doubt, because of their persistence, most vesper sparrows succeed in raising at least one brood each season, and, in spite of many mishaps and tragedies, seem to be able to hold their own.

I found a vesper sparrow's nest that held three young birds on the fourteenth of June one year, when plowing a piece of ground for a late planting of sweetcorn. Naturally, I could not think of plowing the nest under, so left a patch of ground about it unplowed and set a stake near it to mark the spot, thereafter plowing as near it as I dared. The mother sparrow at first flew off whenever I passed the nest, but eventually she became accustomed to the horses and thereafter refused to be disturbed.

A few days later I placed an umbrella blind near this nest from which I hoped to get some intimate glimpses of my musical and useful neighbors, entering it at 2:20 p.m. and remaining for an hour. At 2:25 p.m., one of the parents arrived at the nest with a cabbage butterfly. The eggs of cabbage butterflies produce larvae or caterpillars, commonly called "worms," which are light green in color and very destructive, eating the leaves of cabbage plants, honeycombing the head, littering head and leaves with filth, and doing much harm. Seven trips were made by the parent birds to the nest with food for the young during the hour, a cutworm being fed the last time.

The blind stood within 3 ft. of the nest, consequently I was able to study the appearance of the parent birds to splendid advantage. I could easily make out the white outer tail feathers even when they did not spread their tails, and was surprised at how plainly the bay, or chestnut, on their shoulders could be seen. Their bills were large and conical, but what I noticed most was that their eyes were large, jewellike, and very beautiful.

I soon discovered that both parents fed the young, father working fully as hard as mother. The male invariably fed the young and then sat for no little time beside the nest, alternately watching the youngsters and the blind; and he always seemed much less afraid and suspicious than the mother.

The young sparrows squirmed and moved about a good deal in the nest between feedings, but quickly came to attention and chirped vigorously when a parent arrived with food. The parent birds generally fitted the insect, or other food they had found, to two or three mouths before finding a youngster hungry enough to swallow it at a gulp. If the insect was not swallowed promptly, the parents gave the tidbit to another, this, apparently, being their way of determining which baby was most in need of food.

I noticed that the parents secured most of the insects from the cornfield; and that they found and ate a good many weed seeds themselves while foraging for the young. Sometimes they ate some sand, to enable them to grind the seeds.

The parents fed the young six times the second hour and three the third, for a total of sixteen feedings in three hours, three times offering the young white butterflies or moths, no doubt cabbage butterflies, twice cutworms, twice other caterpillars, perhaps cabbage "worms," and twice ants, great mouthfuls of the latter which they divided among the young. The parents also cleaned the nest several times, thus proving themselves excellent housekeepers.

Chapter 15

THE LARK SPARROW

HERE is one of the prettiest and most neighborly of all sparrows, a bird celebrated both for its good looks and the sweetness of its music. I usually see and hear it for the first time each year in April, when the field and vesper sparrows return, about fields, meadows, pastures, and even in the yard.

The lark sparrow is common west of the Alleghenies, but especially in the upper Mississippi Valley, and spends the winters along the Gulf Coast and in Mexico, but breeds as far north as the Great Lakes. From the Plains, westward, it is supplanted by the western lark sparrow, a subspecies, which is slightly paler in color but otherwise like it. It is either absent or rare in the Alleghenies and Atlantic Coast states, though it may in time extend its range eastward as the horned lark has done.

Sparrows are soberly dressed birds as a rule, the prevailing colors of their plumage being gray, brown, black, and white, though many of them have conspicuous markings of black, white, reddish-brown, and even yellow. The Harris, white-throated, white-crowned, and lark sparrows are perhaps the most conspicuous of the lot, the first having decided black distinguishing marks, the others white field marks.

The lark sparrow is one of the prettiest of the sparrows, its general color above being grayish-brown, streaked with black, while it is white or nearly so below. It has a black spot in the center of the breast, but what interests one most are the markings of the head and tail. The crown is reddish-brown or chestnut with a light median stripe; the ear regions are much the same color; stripes above, and crescents below, the eyes are white; the cheeks are white but bordered with brown below; while the throat is white. In other words, the head has alternate stripes of white and brown that vary somewhat in width.

The tail has white stripes along the sides like that of the vesper sparrow; the two center feathers are dark grayish-brown, whereas the others are brightly tipped with white. When the tail is spread, as it frequently is when the bird is courting, strutting, displaying, alarmed, excited, or feigning injury, it looks like a tiny fan with a pretty white border.

Lark sparrows are confiding and neighborly birds, frequently visiting the yard and singing from the near-by trees. I saw my first one quite a number of years ago when a pair visited the yard. The birds were tame, allowing me to get quite near them, and a glance told me I was viewing a new bird for the first time. The brown markings about the head and the white border of the tail made identification easy. A short while later I found my first nest, hidden in the grass a short distance from a large oak that stood near the top of a sandy, rolling hill. This nest held three cowbird's eggs and two lark sparrow's eggs, the former rather uniformly speckled and spotted, the latter scrawled with black and unlike those of other sparrows.

Lark sparrows make their summer homes in fields, meadows, and pastures, where they nearly always nest on the ground like vesper sparrows. This bird is almost

The nest and eggs of a lark sparrow.

as much of a field sparrow as the vesper sparrow, and the two are often to be found nesting near each other and in similar places. The nest is made of grass mainly but often is lined with considerable hair like those of chipping and field sparrows.

I found a second nest a short time later that had been built in a small field which I was about to plow. I left a wide strip of unplowed ground about the cradle and thus saved it from ruin. The owners, so far as I could discover, did not mind my working near them and went about their affairs as if no one was about. The nest held a cowbird's egg the day I found it, though later it held a clutch of four — three cowbird's eggs and a sparrow's. The cowbird's eggs did not seem to worry the owners and they spent much time flitting and chasing each other playfully back and forth. Their happy-go-lucky ways seemed to indicate they did not realize they had been imposed upon and that all was not exactly as it should be.

The male bird often lowered his wings and spread his tail, strutting and displaying, reminding me of the somewhat similar actions of a turkey cock.

I spent considerable time about the nest after incubation was under way, and the mother became tamer and tamer, so tame, in fact, that, when the young arrived, I was able to stand and watch her at a distance of 5 or 6 ft. without causing her to leave the cradle and had little trouble securing pictures of her while she was brooding. I did not find it necessary to use a blind to get the pictures, though for the nearer ones I used a string for operating the shutter. The location chosen for this nest was a happy one, since it had been built in a cluster of blue-eyed grass. Day after day the pretty blue flowers nodded above the snug little bird home.

The male often visited the yard and sang long and sweetly for us. Two small bur oaks south of the house seemed to be favorite perching places, and he sang almost daily from them for nearly a month. The song is quite unusual and charming, a gushing affair, sometimes short and simple, more often long and complicated, one of the best of all sparrows' songs. The most noticeable thing about it is that buzzing notes are liberally interspersed with the others, as if the bird struck the strings of a stringed musical instrument at regular intervals while singing. The buzzing notes cannot be heard when the songster is in the distance, though pauses tell you when they are uttered. The rest of the song is composed of trills, chees, and many sweetly whistled notes, a series of each, and then the whole quite likely repeated.

A lark sparrow.

Burroughs writes in *Riverby* of a trip he once made to Kentucky and Illinois and states that he saw and heard the lark sparrow for the first time when he reached the Middle West. He speaks of it as "a very elegant, distinguished-appearing bird," but seems to have been disappointed in its song, for he writes of it being "a pleasing performance, but not meriting the praise I had heard bestowed upon it." The present writer, on the other hand, thinks the song merits the many nice things said about it and finds it fully as charming and lovely as ever after hearing it for nearly twenty years. It never gets monotonous and is always interesting and inspiring, charming, sweet, a wonderful song from a lovely bird.

Chapter 16

THE FIELD SPARROW

THE name *field sparrow* is a misnomer, for, as previously stated, this bird (*Spizella pusilla*) is a bush or pasture sparrow, or is it called field sparrow because it never by any chance is to be found about fields? Look for it about the borders of woods, in bushy pastures, open woods, thickets, and the like, where it nests in bushes, small bushy trees, or in the grass and weeds at the base of a stump, tree, or other object.

We have twenty-five or more species of sparrows here in America as well as many finches and other related birds, but many of them are rare or of local distribution. Those I see most frequently are the tree, field, chipping, vesper, lark, song, English, fox, and white-throated sparrows; less often I see the grasshopper, Savannah, white-crowned, and Harris sparrows. The tree sparrow is the only one I see in winter; and the field, lark, chipping, and vesper sparrows are those I have for near neighbors during the nesting season.

Our sparrows constitute a bird puzzle. The tree, field, and chipping sparrows, for example, all have brown crowns, the lark and vesper sparrows have white about their tails, and the white-throated and white-crowned have white field marks about the head. Here we are concerned with the chipping, field, and tree sparrows, which are likely to be confused, for as H. K. Job

A field sparrow on her nest.

remarks, "They are a good deal alike — slender, long-tailed little fellows, with brownish-red crowns."

Fortunately, this puzzle is not hard to solve, since the tree sparrow may at once be recognized by the round dark spot in the exact middle of its otherwise plain breast, and the field sparrow by its pinkish bill. The tree sparrow also has prominent light wing bars and is to be seen during the colder months of the year only, at a time when the other two are absent. The chipping sparrow may be known by its chestnut crown, black forehead, and the light line above, and the dark line running through, each eye. Then, too, the songs of the three are quite unlike and once these are known serve as an additional means of identification.

The field sparrow has a most interesting song; it has a tinkling sound when heard at a distance, the syllable

"dee, dee, dee, dee" repeated over and over with a ringing quality, but has a piping quality and is more rounded
than the syllable indicates when heard at close range.
The song often is short and simple, though again it is
quite long, thus: "dee, dee, dee, dee, dee, dee, dee, dee,
dee-o, dee-o, dee, dee, dee," the first notes being loud and
full, the latter trailing off into silence. This musical little
bird sometimes sings as if inspired, when the courting
and mating season is at its full height and the weather is
agreeable, and then the above may be repeated with
delightful variations until it is hard to imagine that the
elaborate effort comes from the same throat as the more
simple lay.

Field sparrows are among our most numerous bird
neighbors during the nesting season, and sometimes in
a single season, I find as many as eight or ten nests in
gooseberry and raspberry bushes, clumps of dewberries,
juniper trees, and the like, within 2 or 3 ft. of the ground,
either in or near the yard. The only birds as numerous
about the place are the robin, vesper sparrow, brown
thrasher, and redheaded woodpecker.

The field sparrows return to us late in March or early
in April, at about the same time of year as the vesper and
lark sparrows, and then, for several weeks, their tinkling
or piping songs are to be heard early and late, sometimes
in or near the yard, again in the oak grove or far down
the pasture. One or two of the birds nearly always roost
near the house, either in the bur oak that stands 6 ft.
from the northeast corner, or in a spirea bush along the
foundation, and hardly a night passes without our hearing its sweet little song coming from the darkness, a simple "dee, dee, dee, dee" having a ringing quality. It must
sleep lightly, for the slightest noise, such as the distant

barking of a dog, the crowing of a rooster, the opening or closing of a door, a footstep, the rustling of a leaf, and sometimes even, it seems, a whisper causes it to awake and sing a single strain of its delightful song. The time of night makes no difference.

We had many of these little birds nesting either in or near the yard during the spring and summer some years back, when I made a study of the feeding habits of two pairs. We found four nests while they actually were in use and four others later, after they had served the purpose for which they had been built. The children found the first of the former on June eleventh; this was located in a clump of grass at the base of a young oak and held four young birds just out of the shell. I heard some blue jays about this nest eight days later, after the young birds had left it of their own accord, as well as the "chip" alarm notes of the parent sparrows, so hurried to the scene of the disturbance to learn what was up. I hustled the blue jays out of the neighborhood, but found that they had not molested the young birds, which were safely hidden in the near-by bushes. The parents always uttered sharp alarm notes, fluttered about me, feigned injury, and did their best to attract my attention and lure me off whenever I visited the spot for days after that.

I located the next in a bush less than a rod from the house on June first; this held four eggs, but two of them were the eggs of cowbirds. The eggs hatched twelve days later, and then the nest held two young cowbirds and a young sparrow, as one of the rightful eggs failed to hatch. The young cowbirds had the nest to themselves on June nineteenth, having in the meantime crowded the young sparrow from the snug little cradle.

I placed an umbrella blind near this nest to learn how

and what the sparrows fed the young cowbirds. The young interlopers were offered cutworms, caterpillars, bugs, ants, and spiders mainly, but what interested me most were the actual feeding and swallowing of the larger pests. The parents poked cutworms and other large caterpillars far down the throats of their foster children, the latter being so gorged with food they could not swallow the tidbits. True, the young cowbirds made determined efforts to swallow but nearly always failed, the pests slipping part way down their throats and then stopping, so that when the bill was closed part of the insect protruded from between the mandibles. The caterpillar seemed to be caught in a vise when the beak was opened the next time and could neither be swallowed by the young cowbirds nor removed by the sparrows. The sparrows looked at their foster children and their wide-open beaks in a puzzled way, as if trying to determine what was wrong, then grabbed the caterpillar and tried to remove it. After tugging at the pest for a time they let go, and the young cowbird again tried to swallow the tidbit, only to open its mouth shortly as widely as before with the caterpillar still stuck in its throat. Again the sparrows tugged at the morsel, slowly but surely killing and pulling it to pieces and enabling the youngster to finally swallow it.

The next nest was built in a raspberry bush near the yard, and like all field sparrows' nests was a cozy, cup-shaped affair made of fine grass, tiny weed stalks, and the like, and lined with fine grass and hair. After the sparrows deserted this nest because the cowbirds had laid eggs in it, I examined it in detail and found that the birds had used sixty hairs of various lengths and colors when lining it. These same sparrows, I am quite sure, next built in a raspberry bush 3 or 4 rods north of the house, and here, too, cowbirds found and laid two eggs in the nest, but as the owner had two eggs of their own, they incubated all of them. I watched this nest rather closely for fear the young cowbirds would secure most of the food brought to the nest, or crowd the rightful young from it, but nothing happened to warrant any interference on my part. I often watched the parents feeding the young birds, from an umbrella blind which was set near the nest, and they fed the youngsters pretty much in turn, often fitting a caterpillar or other insect to two or three wide-open hungry mouths before finding a youngster hungry enough to swallow the morsel at a single gulp.

Chapter 17

THE CHIPPING SPARROW

THE chipping sparrow, as previously stated, resembles both the tree and field sparrows and hence one of the best clues to its identity is its odd song. However, it is much more likely to be confused with the field sparrow than the tree sparrow, since field and chipping sparrows are about the same size and are with us at the same time of the year.

The chipping sparrow is also known as the social sparrow, chippy or chippie, and hairbird. Hairbird refers to its habit of using hair very freely in the construction of its nest. It is confiding and neighborly and often makes its summer home about our yard, in a bush or vine perhaps, hence is only approached in neighborliness by the robin, house wren, English sparrow, and purple martin.

The chipping sparrow's nest is a small, cuplike jewel case made largely of grass and hair, but neat and attractive though it be, it cannot compare in loveliness with the eggs. The eggs of this bird are among the prettiest of all birds' eggs, being light greenish-blue in color, daintily marked and spotted, chiefly about the larger end, with dark brown. The appearance of the nest, its shape, the materials used in its construction, and its location all make it more or less like that of the field sparrow, but

A chipping sparrow brooding on her nest.

the jewellike eggs should at once tell you when you have a chipping and not a field sparrow's nest before you.

Although the chipping sparrow receives its name from its "chip" call note, its call is far from being a safe clue to its identity, since most sparrows have similar calls. To be sure, some sparrows have call notes that sound more like "cheep" than "chip," while others seem to say "chirp," but these are enough like "chip" to cause the novice considerable trouble. On the other hand, the song of this bird, which Burroughs speaks of as being a "fine sliding chant" — a repetition of its "chip" call — is one of the things by which the friendly little chipping sparrow may be known.

The chipping sparrow migrates in April, usually arriving at its breeding grounds a week or two later than field and vesper sparrows. It is a most valuable bird, since it feeds freely upon garden insect pests of many kinds —

snout beetles, ants, stink bugs, leaf hoppers, plant lice, scale insects, flies, grasshoppers, and caterpillars. More than one third of its food consists of animal matter; in June it is 93 per cent, but this diminishes to 2 per cent during the colder months, when insects are replaced by weed and grass seeds, which constitute nearly two thirds of the yearly food supply.

It was the tenth day of May, a bright, warm, lovely day with happy birds to be seen and heard everywhere. From the fields came the joyous "spring-o'-the-year" of meadowlarks, the "listen to my evening singing" of vesper sparrows, and the varied and inspiring notes of lark sparrows; from the grove came the "cuh-cuh-cuh-cuh" of flickers, the noisy "charr-rr-rr" of redheaded woodpeckers, and the sweet flowing warbles of rose-breasted grosbeaks; while robins sang from the near-by trees, and field sparrows piped and tinkled about the yard. A chipping sparrow had been singing for several days from the bur oak northeast of the house. Occasionally he was joined by his little mate, and the two spent considerable time exploring the grape and ivy vines clinging to some trellises on the west side of the house. Were they thinking of nesting there? If so, we were to have the most useful, gentle, and interesting birds as close neighbors. First, they were to be seen about the ivy vine clinging to the southwest corner of the porch, where a pair of robins had nested the previous year, then about the grape vine on the opposite side of the porch door, and finally about two or three leafy grape twigs or branches clinging to the screen near the northwest corner and forming an ideal nook for a nest. There the little sparrows finally decided to build and at once began carrying fine grasses to the site. At first they did not seem to realize that the screen barred them from the porch and often flew against it when at work.

The mother did the bulk of the work, carrying many loads of grass to the spot, depositing these among the leaves, snuggling down upon them, and working her feet rapidly as she tucked the material into place. The male did his best to help her and brought many fine bits of grass for the nest, laying them on her back, then hurrying off for more. She took the grass he contributed and worked it into the nest together with her own. Strangely enough, it made no difference whatever to the birds whether we were around or not, either on the porch or just outside on the lawn, and they paid but little attention to us and worked away as though we were a thousand miles away. I noticed that whenever the male bird arrived at the nest with a contribution of nesting material that he uttered many low, gentle notes as if talking to her in his sweetest voice.

Sometimes the birds took a brief rest from the nest building, flying from one bush to another as if in play, visiting the bird bath for a drink and a bath, roaming here and there and everywhere, then resuming their work.

The male sang off and on all day but always most freely early in the morning, beginning as soon as it was light. Sometimes I caught sight of the birds in the grass, apparently in search of material, where they seemed to talk to each other a great deal in low tones, as if discussing pro and con the value of the grass for nest-building purposes.

I noticed that the mother sat in the nest for long periods of time the second day, as if pressing the materials into place, getting the nest well shaped to her body, perhaps

The nest of a chipping sparrow.

warming it a bit, so it would be comfortable later on, often snuggling so deeply into the little cup that all I could see of her was her long, slender tail. I climbed to the top of the porch railing late in the day, for a look at the nest, making considerable noise and shaking the vine as I did so, for I was sure neither of the owners was about, since I could not see a bird in the nest. Imagine my surprise, when the mother, who was there after all, stuck her head up. Then I found two very bright eyes watching me over the brim of the cradle, as if trying to get me into a game of peek-a-boo.

The first egg no doubt was laid on the thirteenth day of May, though I did not discover it until the following morning; and, late in the afternoon of the fourteenth, I found a cowbird hovering around that end of the porch with her eyes on the grapevine. I frightened her off and she flew to the east end of the yard, then circled around to the south of the building, finally alighting on the ridge of the house, where she sat watching me with a more or less guilty look. I watched her until she flew off and could not help wondering if she actually knew the location of the chipping sparrow's nest and was planning on laying an egg in it, but finally decided she was only hunting for a suitable nest and had not yet discovered the chippy's cradle.

I was awakened by some fluttering and scolding near the little nest early the next morning. We were sleeping on the porch, about 10 ft. from the nest, and I hurriedly jumped out of bed and made my way toward it. Imagine my surprise and chagrin when I found a cowbird on the nest, looming above it like a sinister black giant. The nest was altogether too small for her, and she looked ridiculous to say the least, but what did the lazy impostor care about that. I stood and watched her for no little time, the owners meanwhile fluttering about the nest and uttering sharp notes of anger and alarm, then moved forward and frightened the black rascal away. I at once looked at the nest and found that it still held the sparrow's but no cowbird's egg. I had frightened her off before she had had time to lay and congratulated myself on this good fortune, but later learned I had been too late anyway, for the sparrows promptly deserted the nest.

My disappointment was keen, as I was hoping to learn much in regard to these interesting and useful sparrows and besides wished to secure some pictures of them. But it was of short duration, for the birds did not leave the neighborhood, as I surely thought they would, and I often saw them fluttering in the grass, splashing in the water of the bird bath, exploring the raspberry bushes, and flying to and fro. Best of all, the male continued to sing from the bur oak. Apparently they were looking for a suitable place for their second nest; and it began to look as if they were going to build it in a raspberry bush northwest of the house, only 2 rods from the one they had deserted.

Five days later I found the second nest exactly where I expected to find it, in the top of a raspberry bush about which I had often seen them meanwhile. I stepped up to the bush to look for the nest and at once saw it, my head, when I made the discovery, being but a foot from it; in the cradle sat the brave little mother. I left at once without frightening her off, since the nest, no doubt, had just been completed, and I did not wish to be the cause of the birds deserting it; on May 24 it held three chipping sparrow's eggs and a cowbird's egg. I wondered, naturally, if the cowbird's egg had been laid by the cowbird I frightened from the first nest, also if the sparrows knew they had again been imposed upon and what they would do about it. I secured a small twig, since I decided then and there to help our little neighbors all I could, and rolled the cowbird's egg out of the nest. The next day I was highly pleased to find that it held four chipping sparrow's eggs.

Incubation now began and on June 3 the first egg hatched; on that date I easily secured some pictures of the mother. The other eggs hatched within a day or two, and, after this momentous event, I secured several additional pictures of the brave mother, for she became tamer than ever, so tame, in fact, that I found I could touch her as she brooded her young and take pictures of her with the camera set a foot away.

We did all in our power to protect the birds and their nest, keeping a careful watch over the bush until the youngsters were almost full grown and able to leave it. I was in the vicinity the day the young birds left the nest and saw them off with the greatest satisfaction, glad to know that another brood of confiding and useful young chipping sparrows had been successfully reared. The happy family lived about the near-by bushes for several days after that and we caught sight of both the young and adult birds again and again. Naturally, at first, the little fellows seldom left the bushes, but in time, as they gained in strength and confidence, they began making longer and longer journeys from one bush to another, or from a bush to a neighboring tree, until they were fully mature and perhaps as capable of caring for themselves as their parents.

Chapter 18

JUNCO AND TREE SPARROW

THE slate-colored junco and tree sparrow — like the downy and hairy woodpeckers, the redheaded and red-bellied woodpeckers, and the chickadee and white-breasted nuthatch — are closely associated in my mind. I find it hard to forget about the other when thinking of one, for they are almost identical in their habits. Both nest elsewhere, but return to this neighborhood in autumn and frequent waste places, weedy fields, roadsides, fence rows, and brushy places about the borders of woods, living almost, if not, wholly upon weed seeds while with us. I see them in the grove, pasture, garden, and fields; and they come to the yard, even to the foundation of the house, and are among our most numerous and confiding winter bird neighbors. Today, March sixteenth, the bird sanctuary is alive with tree sparrows, the little birds flitting and singing everywhere and making it a most delightful place.

The slate-colored junco, or slate-colored snowbird, is our common junco; it is slate-colored above, white underneath, has a white, or straw-colored, bill, and white outer tail feathers. The tree sparrow also is identified easily, since it has a reddish-brown crown, prominent, light wing bars, and a dark spot in the exact center of its plain breast.

Some juncos nest in mountainous regions of the United

A chickadee and slate-colored junco at the food tray.

States, though the true summer home of these birds is
Canada and even Alaska. The tree sparrow also breeds in
Canada but not as far northwestward as the junco. Both
usually delay their southward journey in autumn until
forced to leave their breeding grounds by cold, snow, and
a scarcity of food. I generally see the first ones in October.
Tree sparrows haunt the borders of a near-by stream in
large numbers in late autumn and cheer one with their
"to-lay-it" notes, which Chapman likens to "sparkling
frost crystals turned to music." Slate-colored juncos generally are found farther inland at this season.

Not until winter comes in earnest do I see many of the
two species about my home, however, when they begin
to live about the near-by fields, especially old, weedy fields,
where weed seeds are abundant. The birds live in large
flocks all winter long, wandering from field to field,
waste place to waste place, and pasture to pasture,
wherever weed seeds are to be found. A few stray juncos,

however, are likely to live far from others of their kind and come to the doorstep for crumbs and other food to be found there, roosting in the woodpile or some other sheltered place. These stray juncos are the first to visit our food tray for crumbs, oatmeal, small seeds, and other things we offer them. The tree sparrows are more independent than the juncos and seem to prefer to make or glean their own living, seldom feeding from the tray, whereas the juncos that come remain with us throughout the winter and visit the food tray daily.

The snow becomes deeper and deeper until, late in January, only the tallest weeds project above its surface, and then these birds go from one patch of tall weeds to another and feed upon the seeds of mints, evening primrose, mullein, amaranth, lamb's-quarters, and others. I frequently take walks across the drifted fields and, when I do, find the snow beneath the tall weeds covered with tiny birds' tracks, husks, and seeds, sure signs of the presence of these busy gleaners. When feeding, some of the birds hang to the weeds and thresh and eat their seeds, while others hop over the snow and pick up those that chance to fall.

It is a common sight in many places to see large flocks of birds — usually mixed flocks of juncos, tree sparrows, English sparrows, goldfinches, and perhaps a few cardinals — feasting in patches of weeds after winter snowstorms, a compact group of dark little bodies against a pure-white background, a scene suggesting cold and discomfort perhaps on the one hand, but considerable life and contentment on the other.

F. E. L. Beal made a study of the feeding habits of tree sparrows and estimated that these birds destroy 875 tons of weed seeds yearly in the State of Iowa alone. In making his estimate, Professor Beal estimated ten tree sparrows to the square mile, gave the birds credit for eating ¼ oz. of weed seeds each daily, and assumed they spent two hundred days within the state each year. This he thought a conservative estimate. The tree sparrows are ably assisted by the juncos, the two being our most numerous and consistent weed-seed eaters in winter, although several other species are present, add materially to the total amount of weed seeds destroyed, and should not be overlooked — the goldfinch, cardinal, English sparrow, bobwhite, and some others. No doubt, these birds destroy thousands upon thousands of tons of weed seeds in the United States each year. To the grand total also must be added the weed seeds consumed by several other species in our southern states.

Juncos become musical in the spring, about the time they start for their northern summer home. They migrate in large flocks and trill and twitter in low, scarcely audible tones as they flit about the weeds and bushes. Get near a flock and you may hear some of them say "cheu, cheu, cheu," a contented note, when feeding; but get too near them and they utter sharp clicking notes of alarm.

Chapter 19

THE CARDINAL GROSBEAK

WE WENT fishing the thirteenth of August one year, on one of the wing dams of the Mississippi River. We found bright-red cardinal flowers in bloom everywhere in the lowlands as we approached the Father of Waters. The cardinal birds were not to be outdone that August day, for as we fished we heard a number of them whistling and singing. And we started for home in the twilight with the delightful songs of the birds still to be heard, while everywhere cardinal flowers nodded to us from the deep marsh grass. Though we caught but few fish, the memory of that glorious day still lingers pleasantly with us.

Cardinals, surely, are among our most beautiful and majestic birds with their vermilion-red suits and prominent crests that give them distinction. They are nearly as large as the robin, have reddish bills, and considerable black about the beak; the female is more soberly dressed, the crest, wings, and tail being a duller red, while the red about the body and head is largely replaced by grayish-olive.

The cardinal is a great songster with an arresting and out-of-the-ordinary song. Is there anyone, anywhere, who has this bird for a neighbor who has not listened to his marvelous music? And how can anyone hear his song and not stop, breathless almost, look up, and marvel at

The nest and eggs of a cardinal grosbeak.

that loud, almost piercing, voice of his? The cardinal is a grand opera singer like the brown thrasher, though his song is far from as varied; and, like the latter, he likes a prominent perch when singing, such as the topmost twig of a tall tree. Here is how I interpreted the notes of one of these birds I found in full song late in March one spring: "Whit, whit, whit, whit, whee-u, whee-u! Whit, whit, whit, whee-u, whit, whee-u! Whit, whit, whit, whit, whit!" However, that is but one of the cardinal's songs, of which it has several in its repertoire.

The cardinal prefers to live in wooded regions along streams, where the sun is warmest in winter and where the cold winds lose much of their force. It is to be found in considerable numbers south of a line extending westward from New York City, though it also is a common bird in the upper Mississippi Valley, even as far north as Minnesota and Wisconsin. It is a permanent resident where found, living there throughout the year. I see them more frequently in winter and early spring than in summer, perhaps because the bare trees make their bright-red suits conspicuous. Then, too, they sing most freely in late winter and early spring, wander farther afield, and have a tendency to become secretive in summer, when household cares weigh most heavily upon them.

I frightened a bird from a bush when nest hunting along the wooded shores of a near-by stream one summer. Its alarm notes were unusual, indicating it was a bird whose nest I never before had found. Soon I got a better look at it and noticed it had a stout bill, was reddish, and had a prominent crest. "A cardinal!" I exclaimed. Just then, as if to verify my identification, the male appeared upon the scene, gorgeously dressed in red, a fine crest, and as concerned over my intrusion as his more soberly dressed wife. I found the nest in the bush from which I had frightened her, a frail, shallow affair made of grass, fine twigs, and weeds; it held three light greenish-blue eggs with brown blotches and spots. Find two nests holding eggs, one belonging to a rose-breasted grosbeak, the other to a cardinal, and you will have considerable trouble telling which is which unless you see the owners, for they are built in similar places, resemble each other in size, shape, and materials of which constructed, while the eggs are quite alike in size, color, and markings.

Cardinals are confiding birds, frequently nesting about our homes, especially if these are located near water and contain some suitable bushes and vines. One summer a friend told me a pair of cardinals was nesting in a vine clinging to her porch, just beneath the eaves. The last young bird had left the nest before I got there. We found one in a ditch beside a near-by building; the parents were much concerned about its welfare, perching in the vine, then on a shed, and uttering anxious notes of alarm. We never learned what became of the others, though we assumed they all got safely away. A few days later my friend told me the same birds were nesting in the same vine a second time. This nesting venture met with disaster before long, a cat robbing it one night, destroying the cradle, and perhaps making a meal of the mother. Another friend once told me that cardinals repeatedly nest in a bush in her yard, though all of them are destroyed by cats sooner or later. Cardinals apparently have a hard time rearing a brood, since the nests are built so near the ground they are easily reached by cats and other enemies.

There is another reason why we see more of cardinals in winter than in summer — we have them for neighbors during the former season but not during the latter, since they leave their retreats in river bottoms in late autumn and forage much farther inland, living largely upon weed seeds and wild berries and frequently coming to the yard and feasting upon the frozen grapes to be found about our wild-grape vines and the bluish-black berries of our Virginia creepers. We usually hear them before we see them, for they utter musical "cheeps" when about. This note resembles the common "chip" call of so many sparrows but differs enough so that when heard you know cardinals are about.

Cardinals also come to this neighborhood in winter to feast upon the weed seeds to be found about the gardens, fields, and pastures. Sometimes there are but one or two birds, perhaps accompanied by some tree sparrows,

juncos, goldfinches, and even English sparrows, but more
often there are six or seven of them. When feasting upon
weed seeds, their habits are much like those of the smaller
birds.

Sometimes, too, two or three of the birds visit a spot
in the yard from which we keep the snow shoveled and
supplied with seeds, grain, acorns, and other foods for
the birds. Two, sometimes three, fed daily from this spot
in January and February. In my notebook for January
fourteenth, I find the following: "A pair of cardinals is
now feeding daily on the spot from which we shoveled
the snow and upon which we scatter corn and other
food. The birds take a kernel of corn, work their bills
rapidly, gradually, I suppose, reducing it to pulp so it
can be swallowed, although they seem to make little
headway. Somehow the pressure they put upon the
kernel seems hopelessly inadequate, at least it looks that
way. I notice that the male comes to the cleared ground
at once upon their arrival, but that the female remains
at a distance, perching in a near-by cedar, box elder, or
grapevine. Once when the female came to the spot, the
male darted for her and drove her off. The birds also
feed upon the frozen grapes to be found on a grapevine
trailing along the wire fence east of the house."

I learned that the preceding was not true thirty minutes
later, when the male, who had been hanging around for
some time, apparently waiting for me to scatter some
corn upon the ground, flew to the bare spot near the
window and began to have his supper. He tested the
kernels of corn in some way, rejecting some but retaining
others, then began to work his bill, crushing them so that
small pieces dropped from his bill on either side. The
main part of the kernel was soon crushed and swallowed,

after which he disposed of the crumbs before selecting another. Two English sparrows hovered about him, often picking up the cracked corn as fast as it fell from his beak, as though he were a mill and they the miller waiting for his grist. Sometimes he hopped toward them as much as to tell them to keep their distance. They at once hopped off a short distance upon noting this slight display of impatience but returned to the feast almost immediately. All told, the cardinal seemed about as patient and indulgent as any bird to be found, easily imposed upon by the sly, hardy sparrows.

Chapter 20

THE ROSE-BREASTED GROSBEAK

HAVEN'T you often heard a choked "eek" bird note coming from the near-by trees when roaming through the woods? If so, you have heard the call or alarm of the rose-breasted grosbeak, a common, musical, and loved bird. This note is quite unlike any other bird note to be heard and at once tells you one of these birds is about. Look closely about the crowns of the near trees and you should have little trouble discovering the originator. If the bird is a female, you will find that she looks like an overgrown sparrow with a very stout beak; but, if it is a male, you will discover he is a handsome fellow dressed in black and white and having a large triangular patch of rose red on his breast. The undersides, or lining, of his wings also are rose red, but unless he is raising his wings or flying these cannot be seen.

Remain motionless and the bird may sing for you if it is a male. If it does you will have a chance to hear one of our most remarkable bird songsters. There is a slight similarity between this bird's song and that of the robin, but you will need to have keen ears to detect it. Moreover, you will need to know the songs of both birds well. The song also resembles the better notes of the scarlet tanager and is a rich, flowing, sometimes long-continued warble. Actually, it sounds as if it were produced by a number of carefully attuned, soft, stringed musical instruments, and rivals the better of the classical pieces, sweet, harmonious, delightful. Sometimes it is loud, again low, as if the songster were entirely exhausted or out of breath. Soon it swells forth again, fully as loud and rich as before. What a charming song it is! How melodious! How tender and sweet! This pretty bird sometimes sings when flying from one tree to another — a performance worth going a long distance to enjoy. The female also sings, but far from as often and well as the male. Both parents take turns at incubating the eggs and brooding the young and sometimes sing in a subdued way while thus engaged.

The rose-breasted grosbeak is a common bird in many places, being found in woods, shady retreats along streams and about ponds, in city and country yards, especially if these have some trees and shrubs, and city, county, and state parks. It nests in tall bushes and young trees, usually from 6 or 8 to 15 or 20 ft. from the ground. The nests seldom are as near the ground as those of field and chipping sparrows, catbirds, and brown thrashers nor as high up as those of scarlet tanagers, orioles, and crows. Keep the eyes and attention centered upon bushes, tree-tops, and branches at intermediate heights when looking for the nests of rose-breasted grosbeaks.

The nest is a frail, shallow affair. To be sure, it is considerably better than the tiny rimless platform of the mourning dove, but far from as substantial as the robin's mud and grass bowl, or the cradles of blue jays, crows, catbirds, brown thrashers, and wood thrushes. Nor can it compare with the artistic creations of vireos, Baltimore orioles, wood pewees, chipping sparrows, and many warblers. It is made of twigs, weeds, rootlets, and other similar materials. One that I found and photographed

A young rose-breasted grosbeak.

was so frail and poorly constructed it fell entirely to pieces before the young birds were old enough to leave it of their own accord. The eggs, of which there usually are four, are a pale greenish-blue, spotted with brown.

The rose-breasted grosbeak spends the winters in the West Indies, Central America, Mexico, and northern South America and returns to us early in May. The trees are then budding new leaves, many wild flowers are in bloom, the grass fresh and green, and insects abundant. This bird is wise and returns to its breeding grounds when food is plentiful and the days long, sunny, and warm. What a splendid showing the male then makes when seen against the cool, green background provided by the trees and bushes.

About half of this bird's food consists of vegetable matter and the other half of insects. It is noted for one

The nest and eggs of a rose-breasted grosbeak.

piece of valuable work it does. Few birds eat the Colorado potato beetle, but the rose-breast is rather fond of them, eating the larvae in considerable quantities and thus earning the gratitude of farmers and gardeners, for potato beetles are among the worst insect pests many of them are obliged to combat. The rose-breasted grosbeak is found throughout the greater part of the northern half of the United States in summer, so you should have little trouble seeing and hearing it and thus assuring yourself of a worth-while and delightful treat.

Chapter 21

THE SCARLET TANAGER

HERE is a magnificent creature, a dazzling bit of bird life straight from South America, the male's shoulders, wings, and tail being jet black and the rest of its body bright scarlet. The female, on the other hand, as is true of so many birds, is not as brightly colored as her lord, being greenish-yellow above, yellow below, and having grayish wings. Her plumage makes her inconspicuous among the leaves of trees, favorite haunts of the birds, whereas he makes a remarkable showing and attracts practically all of one's attention. The two look more alike in autumn and winter, though the male still has black wings and tail as in summer.

Tanagers are nearly always to be seen either in or near tall trees in deep woods; they seldom go far from trees except when looking for a change of food, bathing, and securing a drink of water. These brilliant birds once were much more numerous than they now are, since many have been killed for their bright feathers. Still, I succeed in seeing several each year, whenever I visit some woods about the neighboring bluffs, some of our best parks, and natural, wooded beauty spots.

The scarlet tanager has an unusual call, a rather loud "chip-churr," or "chip-burr," which at once tells you when one of the birds is in your vicinity. Look carefully about the leaves and branches of the trees from which the notes seem to come and you should succeed in getting a glimpse of the male, his bright scarlet suit blazing against the cool, green background provided by the leaves. Sometimes a momentary glimpse may be had of this beautiful bird as he flies from one tree to another, since the flights usually are short.

The bird's song is not as easily recognized as its call; it is to be heard far less often, has less carrying power, though there are parts that strongly remind one of the call. It is more like the song of the rose-breasted grosbeak than that of any other bird with which I am familiar, though it has a slight resemblance to that of the robin also. "The most pronounced feature of the scarlet tanager's voice," writes Schuyler Matthews, "is its quality of tone; every note is strongly double-toned or burred." The burred part of the song, or the humming or slurred part, is that which has a resemblance to the call. If you have heard this bird's call, know it well, and then hear a bird's song that reminds you of it, especially about deep woods, you may strongly suspect you are hearing the music of the scarlet tanager.

The nests are frail affairs, made of small twigs, strips of bark, and rootlets, saddled to branches quite far from the ground. From three to five eggs are laid; these are greenish-blue in color but spotted with brown.

I found the nest of a pair of these birds in our oak grove after a long search a few summers ago. Both birds often visited the bird bath, and we often heard their "chip-churr" calls and the song of the male about the tops of the tallest oaks. A redheaded woodpecker chanced to fly to the oak in which the nest was located one day, alighting upon a branch near the top and hammering vigorously at it. The mother tanager darted angrily at it

A young scarlet tanager.

and quickly drove it from the tree with angry notes; nor was she satisfied even then, continuing the chase for some time and being joined by the male. Around and out and in among the trees and branches they chased the woodpecker, the latter circling, dashing this way and that, and eventually hurrying from the vicinity. The mother now flew to the slender branch near the top of the oak from which she had so unceremoniously driven the woodpecker, where she perched for a moment or two beside what proved to be her nest, then resumed her incubating or brooding.

I found a young tanager on the ground not far from this tree after a heavy rain two weeks later; it had fallen from the nest during the storm no doubt. Luckily, it was uninjured, so I perched it upon the dead lower branch of a near-by tree. The mother meanwhile appeared, perched upon the lower branch of another tree, and uttered many anxious "chip-churr" notes. I took two pictures of the little fellow, then left him to the care of the mother, since it was impossible to get it back to the cradle. The parents were to be heard about the grove for some time; consequently, I am quite sure the young bird met with no further mishap.

Chapter 22

THE BROWN THRASHER

THE brown thrasher arrives from his southern winter home about the middle of April or shortly afterwards and is to be heard singing as only a brown thrasher can by the first of May, long, loud, varied, with much zest and vigor, and largely in couplets. Be sure to look about near-by thickets and pastures having large, accommodating brush piles, if you wish to get an early glimpse of him, for he is rather shy, quiet, and secretive at first; he begins to sing in a week or two and then is to be seen perched on twigs or branches near the tops of tall trees, or on telegraph and telephone poles. Later he and his mate are to be found nesting in brush piles, small bushy trees, vines, and even on the ground and the branches of trees.

The brown thrasher is sometimes called the brown thrush. However, it is not a thrush or thrushlike bird like the bluebird, robin, wood thrush, hermit thrush, and veery, but, instead, is a member of the same group of lively singers as the catbird, mockingbird, and wrens. It differs from the true thrushes in being more slender of build and having a longer bill and tail; then, too, his song much more closely resembles that of catbirds and mockingbirds than those of thrushes. In fact, the songs of thrashers, catbirds, and mockingbirds are about as

unlike the songs of thrushes as it is possible for birds'
songs to be.

What does the thrasher say when singing? That usually
depends upon the listener for the thrasher's notes may be
interpreted in many ways. Unfortunately, he sings so
fast it is hard to follow him, though he nearly always
repeats each phrase, which helps. "Plant corn, plant corn"
some folks think he says, but that is not enough, for the
thrasher would vary this in a dozen ways in five minutes.
Here is another common interpretation that also contains
some good advice for farmers, which is worth repeating:

> "Shuck it, shuck it; sow it, sow it;
> Plow it, plow it; hoe it, hoe it!"

Burroughs, on the other hand, interprets the song differ-
ently, writing it thus: "Croquet, croquet, hit it, hit it,
come to me, come to me, tight it, tight it, you're out,
you're out." Does the brown thrasher seem to be proud
of his musical ability and is that why he perches so conspicuously when singing? If so, the following may fit its
efforts: "Whee, whee! Look at me, look at me. Whee,
whee! Can't I sing? Can't I sing?" Toward evening,
when you're tired, perhaps here is what you can imagine
this lovely brown bird to be saying: "Sleep, sleep, go to
sleep, go to sleep; and sleep, and sleep!"

I once heard a thrasher and a catbird that were singing
as if trying to outdo each other. I first heard the thrasher
and climbed a railway embankment to get a glimpse of
him, as he seemed to be bubbling over with song. The
weather had been cold, rainy, and disagreeable the two
previous days, and, as a consequence, we had heard little
of the songs of birds; the thrasher, too, I suspect had had
a good rest, and, because of this and the change in the

A brown thrasher.

weather, felt unusually musical. He flew from the telegraph pole, on which he at first was perched, to a near-by
elm and there continued singing with the same rapidity
and spontaneity as before. I tried to make out what he
was saying, but it was almost impossible, the notes were
uttered so rapidly. Soon a second songster began singing,
a catbird perched among the leaves of a bush a few yards
below me. The catbird seemed to realize he must exert
himself to the utmost to keep up with the thrasher. How
rapidly he moved his mandibles and how the music
poured from his throat! And what a lovely concert I
heard! "Whee! Look at me, look at me!" sang the
thrasher. "There, there" returned the catbird. "Can't I
sing, can't I sing?" asked the thrasher. "Tu, tu, tu, tu,"
replied the catbird.

I found a thrasher's nest one summer that had been
built in a brush pile, and placed an umbrella blind beside
it, from which I was able to watch the owners as they
went about their tasks. They always entered the brush
pile from a point near the ground and then worked their

way up through it to the nest, whereas, when leaving, they hopped to some suitable projecting branch and then flew off. The day was very warm, and the mother spent about half her time shielding the young from the sun and the rest foraging for them, spending from ten to fifteen minutes at the nest and then about as much time securing food. As a rule, she remained at the nest until the male bird got within a few feet of the cradle where he sang in low tones, as if to tell her he had arrived; she now sang in much the same way, as if in reply, then flew off, after which he made his way to the nursery and fed the young birds. He never remained for any length of time but was soon on his way to secure another load of food. After the two birds had spent about fifteen minutes feeding the young, carrying a half-dozen loads or morsels between them, the mother again took her place beside the nest and shielded the young birds from the hot sun.

Once he remained away longer than usual and then the mother and young birds showed considerable uneasiness at his absence, the mother by looking anxiously about, and the young birds by chirping, squirming, and opening their beaks. She waited until her patience was entirely exhausted for the song that would tell her she was at liberty to leave, and then left hurriedly, secured some food, and soon came hurrying back, as if the young were not to be left unguarded a moment. Shortly afterwards he arrived, announcing his arrival with a song, and I could almost imagine seeing her breathe a sigh of relief. Sometimes she spread her wings and tail when he arrived, sang in very low tones, and then flew off.

The adult birds often foraged within a foot of the base of the blind, where they plainly could be heard as they scratched and hunted for insects beneath the leaves; and sometimes the male bird uttered "chick" or "click" notes of alarm, when he heard any noise within it. I estimated that the birds made fifteen trips to the nest with food for the young each hour and that they worked for about sixteen hours each day, from sunrise till sunset or longer, and thus made about two hundred and fifty trips a day. Insects of many kinds, caterpillars especially, made up the bulk of the diet of the young birds, all of which were secured from the ground, beneath leaves and in the tall grass, within a radius of a few hundred feet of the nest.

I once found thrasher's nests in the same vine-draped thorn tree three years in a row, the vine making the head, or crown, dense and tangled and well suited to the tastes of these pretty birds. The site proved an unlucky one, however, because it was in a pasture just outside a large city where cats and boys roamed continually, for all the nests were robbed or destroyed.

Shortly afterwards I found a nest on the ground beneath a fallen branch, then sixteen others, fifteen of which had been built either in bushes or brush piles. The sixteenth nest had been built upon a cluster of tiny branches next to the trunk of a bur oak, about 10 ft. from the ground. I noticed quite a change in the nesting sites chosen by these birds a few years later, finding ten nests in less than a week, all but two of which had been built on the lower branches of trees. The eight nests were in exactly the kind of locations likely to be chosen by mourning doves and had been built, by actual measurement, from 7 to 12½ ft. from the ground where leaves and tiny branches sheltered them from above, since thrashers like a roof over their heads, thus differing from mourning doves who seem to want an unobstructed view of their surroundings. There was a good reason why the

The nest of a brown thrasher. Note that one of
the eggs is undersized.

thrashers had taken to the trees in the neighborhood in
which these nests were located, as it had been denuded
of its bushes and brush piles. I have found many nests
on the ground since then, for brown thrashers nest in
bushes and brush piles when they are available, but are
not averse to trees and even the ground when the occasion demands. In other words, brown thrashers are able
to adapt themselves to changed conditions and modify
their nesting habits when it becomes necessary.

A most unusual nesting place was selected by a pair of
brown thrashers that nested near the yard one year. They
chose a roll of chicken wire that had been laid upon an

oak stump that had a score of vigorous shoots springing from its base. The stump, shoots, and wire had collected a generous amount of dry, brown leaves, and the roll was open at both ends, providing the birds with an entrance and exit, the male invariably using the back opening, or back door, and the mother always entering at the back but leaving at the front.

The owners soon became accustomed to seeing us about the stump and seldom became excited enough to utter any alarm notes. I took a series of pictures of the young and adult birds with the use of an umbrella blind, which I set near the larger, or front opening, that was used by Mrs. Brown Thrasher as an exit. The mother thus passed within a foot or two of the blind each time she left the nest, and, on two occasions, she darted for my hand, giving it a peck and a scratch when I stuck it outside the tent to make some adjustments on the shutter of the camera.

The male bird did more than half the feeding, while the female did most of the brooding; and the greater part of the food was secured within 5 rods of the nest. Many dainty morsels were secured from the grass at the base of the stump. Grasshoppers were caught within a rod or two of the nest, other food was taken from the wood pile which was visited regularly, and caterpillars and the like from the oaks in the grove. I watched the parents feeding the young for less than thirty minutes one afternoon and during that scant half hour eight trips were made to the nest. I noticed, too, when in the blind taking pictures, that the young birds alternately feasted and rested, the entire day being but one long meal, with course following course in quick succession. Brown thrashers, consequently, are of untold value to our agricultural interests, since insect pests of all kinds make up the greater part of the food they give their offspring.

A brush pile is unsightly, especially if it is located in or near the yard, yet we usually have one or more of them about. Though displeasing to the eye, they are of marked service to us, enabling us to have brown thrashers as close neighbors. The birds visit us daily, sing most wonderfully, make good use of the bird bath, and nest on the premises, sometimes in a grapevine clinging to a trellis near the porch door. We furnish the birds with brush piles for nesting places and are rewarded by being treated to grand opera music, having many confidences shown us, and securing many intimate glimpses of them, to say nothing about the economic considerations involved in their continued presence.

My object in placing blinds near the nests previously mentioned was to secure pictures of brown thrashers, though, incidentally, I secured some interesting glimpses of their home life also. I placed the blind near a third nest to learn more about the habits of these birds; this nest had been built in a brush pile near the barn and was the second the owners made near the yard that year, the first also being in a small brush pile.

The birds started building the first nest early in May, the cradle being completed the first week of the month; this held three eggs on the ninth, four on the tenth, and six two days later. Incubation now began, and, in due time, the nest held five young thrashers, since one egg failed to hatch, all of which were successfully reared. I often saw the parents about the brush pile, sometimes making their way to it by a route near the ground, again leaving it more openly, and always found the nest getting fuller and fuller of young bird life whenever I took a

A brown thrasher at the bird bath.

look at it. Finally it overflowed; then the young and adult birds made some bushes near the front yard their headquarters for several days.

Nevertheless, we saw comparatively little of our pretty brown neighbors — that is, considering the location of the nest — because thrashers are shrewd birds and know how to keep the whereabouts of their nests a secret. They do not make any noise near the nest unless it is threatened by enemies; the male never sings in the immediate vicinity; the birds do not fly openly to it, rather follow a route on or near the ground, where their movements are screened by weeds, bushes, trees, and the like; and they try to keep out of sight at all times when in the neighborhood of the precious cradle.

Our neighbors built their second nest in another brush pile near the barn; in a short time this held four eggs, one of which failed to hatch. The young birds arrived late in June. I placed the umbrella blind near this nest, to study their feeding habits and check up on previous observations. How much bird life I discovered about the nest! No signs of bird life could be observed about the brush pile from a distance, but, once inside the blind, how much of interest one found before one's eyes.

I spent three hours within the blind in all, one in the morning, one in the middle of the day, and a third in the late afternoon. The parents made sixteen trips to the nest with food for the young the first hour, fourteen the second, and twelve the third, or forty-two in all, for an average of fourteen per hour. I have always made my observations of the feeding habits of birds at various hours of the day, preferably one in the morning, another at noon, and others later on in the day; those for blue-birds, robins, vesper sparrows, brown thrashers, and meadowlarks being made in this way, since birds do not necessarily feed their young as often at one time of the day as another. At any rate, the data I secured on the brown thrashers this time proved my former observations, estimates, and conclusions to be about correct, or that these birds feed their youngsters two hundred twenty-five times each day, or, at least, make that many trips each day to the nest with food for them.

The parents always entered the brush pile from the far side, gradually working their way to the nest, near which the blind stood, and of which they were constantly a little suspicious, uttering notes of alarm from time to time and craning their necks to get a glimpse of me through the observation hole. I tried my best to keep out of sight, but they always managed to get a glimpse of me and at once began uttering their "clicking," "charr," and whistled "wheu." The young birds began chirping and begging for food when they caught sight of or heard

The umbrella blind beside a brush pile containing
a thrasher's nest.

a parent, crowding and jostling each other to get to the
back of the nest, where they would be at the head of the
bread line, sometimes perching on or hanging over the
rim, their necks stretched and their mouths wide open.

It was impossible for me to determine what the adult
birds fed the young, because they were out of sight most
of the time except when actually cramming food down
their throats. Still, on two occasions, I saw that they had
wild berries, and also noticed that both parents fed the
young. The male bird sang when he arrived near the nest
with food, whereas the mother either remained silent or
uttered notes of alarm; and, though his song was the
same as the one he sang from the treetops, it was sung
in such a subdued way I could scarcely hear it. To all

appearances, he was so happy he could not refrain from singing, but was wise enough to sing in low tones, so his lovely song would not disclose the whereabouts of the nest.

Chapter 23

THE CATBIRD

THE catbird and brown thrasher are likely to be closely associated in the minds of bird lovers, since they belong to the same family, are about the same size, have long, expressive tails, and often nest in similar places. Then, too, the songs of the two birds are so much alike that it sometimes is no easy matter to identify them by their songs alone, both being long continued, varied, and quite unlike those of other birds. The location of the songsters and certain characteristics of the songs often enable one to correctly identify them, however. Catbirds sing from small trees, bushes, vines, and thickets, while brown thrashers choose the tops of tall trees, telephone and telegraph poles, and other equally conspicuous places. The notes of the catbird are not as loud and rich as those of the thrasher, more of them are imitations, and the song has a comic or clownish swing. In other words, the catbird specializes in musical comedy, whereas the brown thrasher is the grand opera singer of the bird world.

The catbird's most common alarm or call is its catlike mew, or "me-ouw," which is responsible for its name; it has another common alarm note also, a low "cluck" or "chuck," which you often hear when you get near a nest.

The catbird frequents thickets and tangles, where it sings its delightful song and builds its nest. Small, leafy trees and bushes generally are chosen for building sites —

thorn-apple trees, wild gooseberry and raspberry bushes, blackberry, grape, and ivy vines — the nests being located in crotches or on clusters of small branches. The cradle is made of small twigs, weed stalks, leaves, and perhaps some string, and is lined with rootlets. The eggs are greenish-blue in color and so in a general way resemble those of the robin, veery, wood thrush, and bluebird.

Many birds have a hard time raising their young, losing their nests, eggs, and young through accidents and tragedies of various kinds, but catbirds seem to be fairly successful in their nesting ventures. There are, of course, reasons for this. Catbirds are fairly large and select safe locations when building their nests; then, too, they are brave and aggressive and defend their nests with vigor when small intruders get near them. Catbirds also frequently nest in thickets and tangles found in marshy places, which are inaccessible to many enemies; and they sometimes nest in bushes in our yards, where they are more or less protected by their human neighbors.

Forty-four per cent of the catbird's food supply consists of insects secured on or near the ground according to studies made by F. E. L. Beal. The rest of its food consists of vegetable matter, in many instances of wild berries. Wild fruits, when they are to be had, are usually taken in preference to cultivated varieties. However, if the catbird does take a little cultivated fruit, it is but securing what it has richly earned destroying insect pests. That the good it does far exceeds the harm is indicated by the fact that it generally nests in marshy thickets and tangled ravines far from our homes. It is not going to travel long distances to rob us of our small fruits when wild berries are to be had much nearer home.

I am very fond of catbirds, my liking being due to their

Young catbirds.

neighborliness, interesting habits, and wonderful songs.
Then, too, they were among the first birds I ever knew,
an acquaintance dating back about forty years to a time
when I lived on a large farm that had a yard well suited
to the tastes of these birds. My home stood a few rods
from the banks of a small brook, and, between the house
and the creek, stood three or four large cottonwood trees,
two white pines, a number of apple trees, a plum thicket,
and two long rows of gooseberry bushes, all of which
appealed to the catbirds, and they nested and spent the
summer near the house. We often heard their catlike
call and alarm notes when playing beneath the trees or
wandering among the bushes; and sometimes we found
a well-hidden nest when picking berries.

Now, we again have a place well suited to the likes of

these birds, since the yard, grove, and our little bird sanctuary have many tangles, thickets, and bushes about them, where they can sing, forage, and nest. A few years back, catbirds stopped off and paid us a visit in the spring when migrating and also made brief calls after the nesting season and feasted upon our berries and took advantage of our bird bath, though they did not actually nest about the premises. Then, however, a pair decided to nest in a thicket west of the house, the birds arriving early in May and spending much of their time about the chosen spot. They sometimes visited the bird bath and investigated the vines clinging to the trellis on the west side of the porch. The male seemed especially interested in them, and many a morning we were awakened by his rollicking, varied, and comical song. Indeed his song at times was so loud and had such a queer comic swing that it was the cause of much pleasure and amusement. Often it would die down, as if the songster were moving off, then it would burst forth as loudly as ever.

The birds built at least three nests in the thicket that year, and succeeded in raising but one youngster, I am quite sure. There were many heavy rain and wind storms that summer and one nest after the other was blown to the ground and ruined. No sooner was one nest destroyed, however, than the birds started another in a near-by bush or oak seedling. The male advertised the fact that a new nest was being built and eggs deposited in it by singing more freely and with greater abandon than he did at other times.

The birds returned on the fifth day of May the following spring, and we were delighted to hear their call notes and to catch glimpses of their dark gray suits about the bushes in the thicket, where they had nested with such

A cowbird's egg in a catbird's nest.

little success the previous year. The birds spent most of their time about the thicket for several days, feasting, resting, calling, though they also visited the bird bath and occasionally inspected some vines near the porch, where the male sang as the examination proceeded. I was sure the birds were going to nest in the thicket, and soon noticed that the mother was busy carrying grass, weeds, straw, and other materials to it one day. She edged about and seemed suspicious, tried to keep out of sight, dodging behind bushes and trees and flying near the ground. I discovered the location of the nest by watching her closely; it was being built in a bush about a rod from the drive, where we were able to get a good look at both cradle and bird whenever we used the road. It seemed to be ready for use about the middle of the month, and the mother was in it when I passed on my way to town. She began spending practically all of her time in the nest a few days later, clearly indicating it then held four or five dark greenish-blue eggs. I did not dare to go near the nest to see what it held, however, for fear of alarming the owners and causing them to desert it; instead, I was content to glance casually that way and to keep watch of affairs at a distance.

One day the children came running into the house, greatly excited, to tell me that the mother was carrying eggs from the nest. As it was not yet hatching time, I was sure something had frightened the birds and caused them to desert their nest. How else could one explain such queer actions? The children stoutly maintained they had not been near the nest, so I decided to continue watching things from a distance; and, a day or two later, was relieved to find the bird in her nest as usual. Not until the eggs were about due to hatch did I venture near the bush for a look at the nest, only to find that it held but two eggs. I concluded that the other eggs had been accidentally broken in some way, and that the mother had been carrying the shells away the day the children told me they had seen her carrying eggs from the nest.

The young birds made their appearance the second week in June. A few days later I noticed that the nest was tipped to one side and was about to fall to the ground. When I reached it, I found that it held but one young bird, the other having fallen to the ground and perished from exposure and starvation. I straightened and propped up the nest as best I could and thus saved the life of the last youngster. Catbirds and thrashers frequently nest in berry bushes, but unless the bushes are

The nest and young of the catbird.

large and have many shoots and branches they seem to have considerable trouble anchoring them properly.

Catbirds have nested near the house the past eight years also, usually only a pair, raising one or two broods of young each season and nearly always building one nest which they desert before egg-laying time.

Chapter 24

THE HOUSE WREN

THE house wren, in spite of its diminutive size, is one of our most remarkable singers; that is, if we consider the strength and volume of his efforts and not the variety of the notes. How each cheerful warble comes rolling or bubbling from his throat rapidly followed by the next, how rapidly his mandibles move, and how long he can continue singing without seeming to tire.

Every city and town seems to have its share of these little songsters nesting in houses of all kinds and descriptions made and set out for them by kind people. They are so different from most other birds that one needs only to note their size and the position of the tail to correctly identify them. And one warble of his bubbling song is enough to tell you that the little bird hovering about a can or box in your neighbor's yard is a house wren. I have heard the songs of a dozen different wrens coming from a dozen different back yards during a single short walk. If, as frequently happens, I take my walks along the same streets and in the same direction, I soon learn where I may expect to hear the songs of the little fellows.

I once found a house wren building a nest in a large tin can lying on the top of a roll of discarded wire fencing on a rubbish heap. The can was 3 by 5 in. wide and 10 in. deep and had a hole in one end just large enough for the bird to enter. When I discovered him, he was

The post used by wrens for nesting.

hard at work filling it with tiny twigs and bits of hay and straw. I stopped and watched him work and saw him carry at least twenty loads into the can. Sometimes he attempted to carry sticks in crosswise and, when so doing, rocked his queer house, which was nicely balanced upon a strand of wire and thus served as a teeter-totter as well as a summer home. I soon saw he was a brave little fellow and that I could get near the can without frightening him; and sometimes he stopped working long enough to sing his happy song over a few times. I found him busily singing and working the next two or three days but absent the next. He returned after an absence of about a day and then had Mrs. House Wren with him. She made several trips to the can with nesting material while I was there, whereas he kept things lively with his bubbling music.

I concluded the pair had now gone to housekeeping in earnest and hoped for many pleasant hours watching affairs about the old can, but their nesting venture was soon over, for one day I found the can out of place and deserted. Just what had happened was hard to say. A gust of wind may have tipped it over, or a wandering boy meddled in some way and thus ruined this bird home.

One year, after an absence of ten months, we returned home about the middle of June and found that the birds had taken complete possession of the place. All bird sounds — both calls and music — seemed loud and strange to us at first, coming, as they did, from trees, posts, and bushes so near the house. The bobwhite, brown thrasher, and meadowlark were awake and singing very early the first morning as if to welcome us. They seemed to like the yard, grove, fields, and pasture whether there were folks about or not, whereas the bustling house wren seemed to have other ideas. Apparently he did not like the place when it was deserted and consequently did not make his appearance until we had been at home a few days. Then, one day, I awoke and heard his song, and he continued to sing unceasingly until well toward noon. Then there was a long lull while he explored a pile of lumber and inspected an old paint pail, apparently searching for a suitable nesting place. I hastily constructed a box from an old tin can and fastened it to a post near the lumber, then made another and nailed it to the wall of the shed.

He found the can fastened to the shed almost at once

and kept busy for several days filling it with small twigs, weed stalks, and bits of straw and grass. He always sang unceasingly during the morning hours, but quieted down toward noon, working harder and singing less; and he sang and worked but little during the afternoon, spending most of his time on or near the ground, where he no doubt was feeding and resting because hungry and tired.

One morning I heard his song as usual, then noticed it ceased and that he was nowhere to be seen. I saw no more of him that day and was a little afraid he had deserted us, but heard his song as usual early the next morning and found that he had his little wife with him. She seemed more timid than he and tried to keep out of sight as much as possible.

She kept busy for several days building a nest in the can, while he spent most of his time gaily singing. He never carried anything to the tin can after she arrived, apparently turning the housebuilding and housekeeping entirely over to her, though he sang more freely and with greater abandon, in an effort to encourage her, no doubt. He seemed intensely interested in how the work was progressing, however, and once I caught sight of him leaning far out over the edge of the shed roof, intently watching the can, out of which she shortly emerged.

The nest was finally completed, and then the birds took things easier. Then, one day, I found she had disappeared, though he continued singing much as before. He remained with us for more than a week after that, singing and making things cheerful for us, then he, too, disappeared.

A week or so later the same birds or two others appeared, spending most of their time about a brush pile in which a pair of brown thrashers had previously nested

The nest and eggs of a house wren.

and reared a brood. The wrens made a hole in the foundation of the discarded thrasher's cradle and in it fashioned a cradle of their own. This no doubt was done largely for the pleasure of the work and not because they expected to take up housekeeping in earnest, for it then was late July and some birds were beginning to congregate in flocks in preparation for a long journey southward.

I usually begin looking and listening for this little bird late in April. Seldom, if ever, does he disappoint me by being late. I usually hear and see the first one about a small yard a short distance off, where the renter has long maintained a wren house for a pair of the birds. As I near this yard at wren-arrival time I hear his bubbling warble and a moment later catch sight of him, tail pointed skyward, as he hops in the grass, perches on the branch of a tree, or teeters on the wren box fastened to a corner of the house.

We have long had wrens for close neighbors, although, for several years, we had trouble inducing them to remain with us, most of them acting like the pair or pairs previously mentioned. The first pair to actually nest on the premises chose a knothole in the wall of the hen house for an entrance and built a nest in some litter used for insulation. Then for a few years again the birds nested elsewhere. Some years we saw little of them in the neighborhood, but, more often, a male visited us, sang, bustled about, and inspected every box and hole about the place. Sometimes he found a mate and the two spent no little time with us before leaving and nesting elsewhere.

Finally, I secured two pieces of hollow birch and made wren boxes out of them. The first was part of a hollow branch 9 in. long and 3 in. in diameter. I nailed small pieces of lumber over the ends and thus gave it a roof and floor, and a pair of wrens nested in it and successfully raised a brood of youngsters. The next winter woodpeckers destroyed this box, since the wood was partly decayed and very soft and they loved to hammer at it. The other piece was the same length as the first but 7 or 8 in. in diameter. I split it, nailed a board across the back of the half used, gave this an entrance hole, roof, and floor, and fastened it to a corner of the shed. Wrens have nested in this rustic box several times. Woodpeckers drilled a hole in it also, after it had been in use two years, the new hole being on the left side near the floor. The wrens filled the bottom with twigs, thus plugging the lower hole, and continued using the original entrance. This box is still fastened to the shed and always reminds me of our little neighbors when I pass it, for twigs still protrude from the hole the woodpeckers made.

We tore up an old fence one April, removing the wire and taking up the posts. The posts were hauled to the yard, sorted, and either saved or placed on the woodpile. Among the discarded posts was one that was hollow, the hole being full of twigs like those used by wrens when nest building. Whenever I find a post, log, branch, or tree trunk that contains a cavity of this kind I save the hollow part for a bird box. The hollow was near the bottom, at about ground level, so I reversed the ends and set the post in the ground a short distance north of the house, the entrance hole now being 3 ft. up.

True to schedule, the wrens arrived about the first of May. How the male sang, flitted about, searched, and worked! Soon his mate arrived, and the two began carrying twigs into a hollow-branch bluebird box southeast of the house, no doubt nesting there, though I was too busy to keep a close watch over their affairs, then began hovering about the post I had recently prepared for them. How the male sang and flitted about that hollow post! Eventually things quieted down. The male, to be sure, still sang freely about the old post, but nothing was to be seen of his mate. Then, one day, when I visited the vicinity, the mother appeared in the entrance hole, uttered notes of anger and alarm, and flew to a near-by tree, where she was joined by her mate, both birds chattering and scolding as long as I remained.

Soon there were youngsters in the nest, and the parents were kept busy early and late feeding them. I have never

been successful in photographing wrens, so concluded
here was my chance. The young were quite large by the
fifth of July and frequently were to be seen at the entrance hole. On the sixth I placed a blind beside the post,
leaving it there overnight to get the birds accustomed to
it. The next day when I arrived with the camera all was
quiet at the post. The parents were not to be seen, and
no young wrens appeared at the entrance. I had come too
late — the nest was empty. I found one youngster in a
near-by mulberry, another in a box elder, and still others
about some young oaks. Thereafter for more than a week
we saw much of the young and old birds, a happy family
that gave us much enjoyment. Naturally, I was keenly
disappointed about not getting any pictures, but a large
and happy family of wrens about the yard is better than
many pictures, isn't it?

Chapter 25

THE WHITE-BREASTED NUTHATCH

THREE outstanding characteristics of the white-breasted nuthatch are his confiding disposition, his ability to make his way down and around the trunks and branches of trees, and his neatness. His suit is sleek and clean and he always makes a good appearance. You can nearly always get quite near to him while he is busy about a tree, not because he is unaware of you, for he is always wide awake and alert, but because he trusts you. He stops and watches you and then, as likely as not, greets you with a friendly "twit" or "How do you do!" Off he starts again in a moment, head first down the tree until he reaches the ground, then flies well up another and makes his way down it in turn. He creeps along the underside of a branch as easily as along the upper, with a good many twists, turns, and other gymnastic exercises for good measure.

How is our bird dressed and why does he make a splendid appearance? Gray suit, white vest, and black cap! There you have it, though the white of the breast extends to the throat and cheeks, the black on the crown to the nape and extreme upper back, while the wings and tail, which are mainly black, are brightened with white. The white-breasted nuthatch is a short, chubby bird with a long, sharp beak and a short, square tail. That beak enables it to dislodge insect pests of many kinds from cracks and crevices in the bark. The toes are long and equipped with long, sharp claws that enable it to hang to the undersides of branches as easily as a fly hangs to the walls and ceilings of our homes.

The notes of this bird are so unlike those of other birds that they at once tell you when there is one about. "Ank, ank," or "yank, yank," he calls in grunting tones as he makes his way down a tree, the throat swelling and pulsating as the notes are uttered, though the mandibles may not move at all. The "ank, ank," consequently, must be produced entirely in the throat, and this little acrobat, I suspect, would make a first-rate ventriloquist had he a suitable dummy. He can sing, too; perhaps not as wonderfully as many birds, but pleasantly, nevertheless, especially when the song is heard on a cold February morning, when little or no other bird music is to be heard. He usually perches quietly near the top of a tree when singing; and "kwee, kwee, kwee, kwee" is what he seems to say; and he talks in low twits when in the company of other birds, or to a human being, whom he eyes intently.

The white-breasted nuthatch remains with us all year, like the downy and hairy woodpeckers, cardinal, blue jay, and bobwhite. Make a food tray and fasten a suet stick to one corner, set it up in the yard and keep it supplied with food if you want it for a winter neighbor and want him to visit you when other birds are scarce, since it is one of the easiest of birds to attract to the yard in winter by means of a little food. Beef suet makes an ideal food for this little bird, since it lives largely upon insects it finds about trees, though it will also eat oatmeal. When he visits your food tray be sure to notice how he seems to skate over the bottom and how little he fears you.

The white-breasted nuthatch.

A pair of these birds visited us regularly one winter, coming daily to our food tray, which was located near an east window, and feasting upon suet and oatmeal. The male was boss and always drove his little wife off until he had had his fill, darting spitefully at her if she dared to come to the tray while he was there. All winter long she was obliged to keep at a respectable distance, inspecting some near-by tree, a post in the fence, or perching upon a branch until he left the tray. His attitude toward her changed and gallantry again prevailed with the coming of milder weather in February. Then he talked to her a good deal in low "twits," allowed her to feed beside him, and even offered her choice morsels of food from time to time.

The white-breasted nuthatch nests in holes and cavities in trees; these may be enlarged or changed slightly and then lined with feathers, fur, and other soft materials. From five to eight white or pinkish eggs spotted with brown are laid by the mother. The young birds make interesting subjects for photographs when nearly full grown, and many are the excellent pictures secured of families of them by nature photographers.

Chapter 26

THE WOOD THRUSH

THERE is something inspiring yet peaceful and restful about the song of the wood thrush. I often fished a deep pool near the east shore of a large tributary of the Mississippi River one summer. I usually went there in the late afternoon, and nearly always heard the songs of some wood thrushes that frequented the wooded west shore. There were long rests between the songs of the birds, as if the songsters had all the time in the world. Clearly the birds sang "come to me," or "a-e-o-lee" the notes having a flute- as well as bell-like quality. Then I realized more than ever the charm of the song of the wood thrush, which has inspired and charmed so many.

The wood thrush has some famous relatives and is closely related to the bluebird and robin, our harbingers of spring, which are thrushes or thrushlike birds. Thrushes have spotted breasts and though robins and bluebirds do not have spotted breasts their young are thus adorned, giving them a thrushlike appearance. Other relatives of the wood thrush are the gray-cheeked thrush, olive-backed thrush, veery or Wilson's thrush, and hermit thrush. The gray-cheeked and olive-backed thrushes are rare birds, to be seen mainly at migration time in our eastern states, but the veery and hermit thrush are much more common, even in the interior of the country.

The wood thrush is the largest of our thrushes with the exception of the robin, the latter being 10 in. in length, the former 8 in. It is reddish-brown in color above, but much brighter on the back of the head than elsewhere, and its breast is heavily marked with black spots.

The favorite haunts of the wood thrush are the wooded shores of streams, ponds, and marshes, though it also is to be seen about cities and towns, where it sings from the shade trees and gleans food from the yards, and sometimes far up large, deeply wooded hills. A large cone-shaped hill stands near my home, whose slopes are heavily wooded with oak, poplar, linden, walnut, and other trees. Each year I hear the bell-like songs of wood thrushes about it and frequently find the nests of the lovely songsters.

The wood thrush migrates late in April, reaching its nesting grounds early in May, and begins to nest about the middle of the month. Our bell bird remains with us until about the first of October, five glorious months in all, then leaves for its winter home south of the United States.

The nests of wood thrushes usually are built in the forks of trees, from 4 to 10 ft. from the ground, and are bowl-shaped and substantially made of mud, grass, weeds, and leaves. They are shaped much like the nests of robins, but are slightly smaller. Many of them are made almost entirely of reeds, weeds, and mud, being rather neat and artistic, though others are made almost wholly of leaves and mud. I once found four nests about the slopes of the cone-shaped hill that had been made almost entirely of mud and leaves; from one of these I took nearly sixty dry, brown leaves. The nests are lined with grass and rootlets; and the three or four eggs are greenish-blue,

Two young wood thrushes.

slightly smaller but much like those of the robin.
The song of the wood thrush is worthy of a few more
remarks. When heard at a distance, the pleasant bell-like
"come to me," or "a-e-o-lee," is all that can be heard;
but, when one is near the songster, these notes are found
to be preceded and followed by others that are not so
pleasant and musical. The song opens with two hard
"chucks," or "clucks," and ends with a "cheer," "trill,"
or other note. Its song may be written in the following
ways: "Chuck, chuck, a-e-o-lee, cheer"; "chuck, chuck,
a-e-o-lee, trill"; and "chuck, chuck, a-e-o-lee, z-z-z." Here
we have three songs, all of which, it will be noted, have
different endings. The call of the bird is a "chirp" that
sounds a good deal like the common call of the robin;
and its usual note of alarm is a sharp, explosive "pip,
pip," or "pit, pit."

I was on a nest-hunting trip the 25th of May one spring, along the banks of a small stream about a mile southeast of my home, in one of those lovely bird nooks one sometimes runs across. The first nest I found belonged to a red-winged blackbird, that had been built in a lilac bush growing in an old deserted farmyard. The yard bordered the stream on the north and hence the bush was suitably located for the nests of water-loving birds. A few moments later I met a wood thrush face to face; it uttered a few sharp "pip, pip" notes of alarm, turned, and hurried off, perhaps to join her mate whose inspiring "a-e-o-lee" song I heard coming from a wooded thicket up the bank. I began to search for the nest, which I was sure was located near me, soon finding it in a box elder. It was a typical wood thrush's nest made of weeds, reeds, grass, and mud and located about 4 ft. from the ground. I took a look within it, to see what it held, and found three greenish-blue thrush's eggs and a white, speckled cowbird's egg.

A few days later I tried to secure pictures of one or both of the owners of this nest, but though I worked long and faithfully, trying two or three devices, I failed to get a single worth-while shot. Later, when working my way through the thicket to the east, I met some boys armed with air guns and 22 rifles who were shooting at every bird and animal coming their way. Since the wood thrush's nest was on the opposite shore, I did not fear for its safety; but, upon visiting the place a day or two later, I found my nest had been destroyed. My disappointment was keen, since I had high hopes of securing some good pictures of these pretty and useful birds.

June the second again found me on a nest-hunting trip, when I visited the wooded slopes of Sugar Loaf,

The nest and eggs of a wood thrush.

a splendid cone-shaped hill. On my way I passed a sandy
bank where I had once found a lone bank swallow's nest.
Part of the bank had caved away just previous to that
visit, leaving the swallow's nest in plain sight. I found a
bird in the nest and picked it up, thinking it a youngster.
Imagine my surprise when I saw that the bird was sitting
on a number of pure-white eggs. Then the truth dawned
upon me: the bird I held in my hand was an adult bank
swallow. I opened my hand, when with a joyous twitter
or two the bird flew off and alighted upon a near-by
telephone wire. On this trip, too, the bank swallow's nest
held something of interest, for in it I found four young
white-footed mice.

The first nest I found about Sugar Loaf Hill was that
of a wood thrush, near the top of a small, crooked elm
standing in a lovely shaded ravine that was thickly dotted

A brooding wood thrush.

with Jack-in-the-pulpits, trilliums, and rue anemones. I found a catbird's nest that held five eggs and another wood thrush's nest a little farther on, the latter in a white birch, less than 4 ft. from the ground.

Later I found two more wood thrushes' nests on the opposite side of the hill, making four such nests in all for the day. Needless to say, perhaps, I was well satisfied with my day's work. There were sitting or incubating birds in all the nests; only one of these left her eggs because of my intrusion. All the nests had been built partly of dry, brown leaves; in fact, two of the nests were very large and bulky and looked as if made wholly of this material.

The second nest proved of unusual interest, because the sitting bird proved very tame. I returned to this nest on June fourth with my camera, working my way slowly toward the birch, until I was less than 6 ft. away, where

The wood thrush or "bell bird."

I took a picture of the brave bird, then advanced a little
and took another, and then still another. I now circled
the tree and, from another angle, took two more before the
bird fluttered from her nest. Soon she was back, however,
posing for additional pictures, and, before I left, I had
secured a dozen time exposures of her. She flew off again
after the last exposure and I looked at the nest, finding
that it held a young wood thrush just out of the shell and
an unhatched egg. I had arrived for my pictures at the
critical hatching time, which accounted for the way the
mother had braved me and my camera. Under no circumstances must she allow the unhatched egg to become
cold and thus kill the young bird within it. It was mother
love for an unhatched youngster that had kept her on the
nest in the face of apparent danger. However, the strang-

est thing of all was that the unhatched egg was not the egg of a wood thrush, for it was white and rather profusely marked and spotted with darker shades — the egg of that feathered shirker, the cowbird!

Chapter 27

THE BLUEBIRD

IT IS March! High overhead a bluebird is winging his way northward with glad tidings, uttering a mellow "tru-ly," or "teer-a-lee," as he flies by. Not long afterwards, say in a day or two, you hear the bird's delightful notes coming from the pasture fence and you hurry outside to get a glimpse of it. His reddish breast and his lovely blue upper parts show to advantage as he goes to and from some morsel of food he has discovered. How beautiful the bird seems! The bird again utters his welcome notes, and you listen intently and feel an inexpressible joy. Bluebird is back and spring again is here!

The pleasure of seeing the first bluebird of spring is an experience reserved to those living north of this bird's winter haunts. However, folks living in our southern states, where this bird spends the winters, have the pleasure of seeing and hearing it during the winter months, a pleasure many northern people would thoroughly enjoy.

The bluebird belongs to the thrush family, being a near relative of our old friend, robin redbreast, the veery, and wood and hermit thrushes. Young bluebirds, like young robins, show this kinship by having spotted breasts. Bluebirds differ from the other members of the thrush family by nesting in holes in stumps, posts, and trees and in being easily attracted to the yard by means of suitable nesting boxes.

Nesting boxes for bluebirds should measure 4 by 4, or 5 by 5, by 8 in. and should have entrance holes 1½ in. in diameter. Boxes or houses covered with bark prove much more attractive than painted ones, since the former more closely resemble their natural nesting places. However, I have found that better boxes may be made from hollow posts, stubs, branches, and tree trunks. In fact, boxes made from such materials are the best obtainable for attracting bluebirds to the premises during the nesting season.

I have about a dozen such boxes about the premises at the present time, one or two made from hollow posts, at least four made from hollow tree trunks, and the rest made from hollow stubs and branches. When I find a hollow post, stub, branch, or tree trunk, I remove the hollow portion with a saw, usually a piece from 12 to 20 in. in length, close the top and bottom if necessary, and fasten it to a building, tree, or post in or near the yard. Sometimes a piece 6, 8, or 10 ft. in length may be taken and the whole set in the ground like a post.

Bluebird boxes of this kind are natural nesting sites, easily made, and prove very attractive. Generally all the tools one needs to make one is a saw and a hammer. If the hollow runs the length of the tree trunk, post, or branch, the top and bottom should be closed. The part taken should include the old entrance hole; otherwise it will be necessary to make one.

Bluebirds have at one time or another used most of our rustic bluebird boxes for nesting. The first few years they nested in only two or three I made from hollow posts, then changed and occupied two they never before had used. One of these was a hollow branch 8 ft. long which I secured and set in a thicket north of the house, the other a hollow chunk of wood I cut from the trunk of an oak and placed west of the house, fastening it securely to a pole set in the ground. The favorite box, however, one of the first I ever made, was taken from a hollow post in which bluebirds to all appearances had previously nested, since it held the remains of a discarded nest. I cut the hollow portion from this post, nailed boards over the top and bottom, and wired it securely to a post a rod northeast of the house.

A pair of bluebirds had been hovering about the yard for some time that spring, no doubt looking for a place to nest. Shortly after I had my queer nesting box in place, they took possession of it, throwing out the old nest and building a new one of their own. Two weeks later I found that there were eggs in the nest.

The nest held half-grown youngsters the middle of May, when I studied their feeding habits rather carefully and learned that the parents were feeding their young largely upon cutworms. They thus no doubt saved large numbers of cultivated plants from the ravages of the pests, since a few dozen cutworms are capable of destroying scores of cabbage, tomato, melon, corn, and other plants daily. And these bluebirds were feeding scores of cutworms to their young each day, leading me to wonder how many they fed them in a week and how many other bluebirds in the neighborhood were feeding their young on a similar diet. There were five young birds in the first brood, which left the nest on the 22nd and 23rd days of May. Our bluebirds used this box or house for their second brood also, the mother in this instance laying four pretty blue eggs, all of which

A male bluebird at a nesting box with food for the young.

hatched. The four youngsters met with no mishap and in due time got safely away, so nine young bluebirds in all were thus successfully reared in this box the first year.

The parents, and young birds, too, took a great liking to the old post home and were often to be seen about it the remainder of the summer and much of the autumn; and they frequently drove off any redheaded woodpeckers and other birds that happened to wander near it.

Our bluebird neighbors arrive from their southern winter home early in March. Sometimes, however, they return the third week in February, and they remain with us until November.

They usually visit our rustic bird boxes and claim them as their own as soon as they arrive in the spring; and, though they usually do not nest until several weeks have elapsed, they remain in the immediate neighborhood meanwhile and guard their proposed nesting places from the intrusions of other birds, waging war upon blue jays, English sparrows, the friendly and confiding chipping sparrows, field sparrows, vesper sparrows, but mainly upon the thrifty and independent redheaded woodpeckers who are interested in hollow posts, tree trunks and branches, so do not overlook our bluebird boxes. The bluebirds, however, are aggressive and protect their boxes with vigor and are hardly ever deprived of them by other birds.

The feeding habits of bluebirds are very interesting. The adult birds live almost entirely upon insects and other small forms of animal life they glean from the ground during the eight months they are with us. They also feed their young entirely upon such foods, working from dawn until it is dark at night, finding and giving the youngsters caterpillars, butterflies, moths, bugs, spiders, crickets, grasshoppers, and other small creatures. Cutworms are destroyed in large numbers in early spring and grasshoppers later in the season.

I have taken many pictures of bluebirds from umbrella blinds, of which they usually are but little afraid. Sometimes the male has proved the braver, other times the female.

One year our lovely neighbors arrived from their winter home the 14th of March. They at once visited the nesting boxes, first one, then another. Eventually they reached the favorite box, looked inside, surveyed the landscape, and then looked inside again, bobbing or tilting forward

The nest and eggs of a bluebird in our paper box.

much like woodpeckers. Finally one went inside and looked it over more carefully, came out again, and the other inspected the old home. Apparently both found it much to their liking, much as when they last saw it, and their notes had a satisfied and joyful quality. The male seemed especially pleased and raised and spread and fluttered his wings as if very happy. This "twinkling" of the wings is one of the delightful things about the bluebird.

For several weeks the birds guarded their boxes carefully from the intrusion of other birds. On one occasion they waged war upon some blue jays that settled in the ivy vine draped over the favorite box. The bluebirds darted for the larger birds with angry notes, snapped their bills threateningly as they passed them, turned and then swooped again. And they continued scolding, dart-ing, and snapping their bills, taking turns at attacking and abusing the enemy, until the jays flew off. Later they were forced to make war upon some English sparrows that took a liking to one of the boxes, and occasionally they drove off other birds, redheaded woodpeckers especially.

The first nest was not completed until the last week in April; on the 28th it held two pretty eggs, but after that no more were laid, which is quite unusual, as blue-birds nearly always lay four or five. Incubation was soon under way, and then I often saw the male carrying food to the box for his mate. He often perched on a near-by post with a cutworm or other pest in his beak, made sure no intruder was near, then flew to the entrance hole, looked the premises over, both inside and out, and entered the box. In a few moments out he came again with an empty beak.

The nest held one young bird on the 17th of May, as one of the eggs failed to hatch. I rapped gently on the box and the little fellow raised his head and opened his mouth widely. What a sight a hungry young bird makes when it hears a noise it thinks is made by a returning parent!

The mother in time became so tame that upon two occasions she remained on her nest when I visited the post. Each time I was obliged to look long and carefully within the dark interior before seeing her, first getting a glimpse of her bright eyes, then her bill, and finally her tail.

Late in May I found her perched on a near-by post with a cutworm in her beak. The insect was alive and twisted and squirmed in its efforts to get away, describing several complete circles before she became tired of its antics and struck her bill sharply against the post to quiet it. This had the desired effect, but only for a few moments; and before she ventured to the box she was obliged to repeat the punishment several times, and I doubt if the pest quit twisting and squirming before it reached the young bird's crop.

Though our pretty and useful neighbors raised only one youngster the first time, they were more successful the second, when they nested in a box southeast of the house and had a lusty family of five. The mother now became tamer than ever and rarely left her nest when we came near the post. Perhaps, eventually, she will become tame enough to allow us to touch her and will honor us by taking food from our fingers.

I made a similar rustic bluebird house a year or two previous to making the favorite box, and fastened it to a post north of the house. Bluebirds nested in it the first year, but, I had to move it to a bur oak south of the house as soon as the young were safely out of it, because a group of curious children bothered it. Here it also was used by a pair of the birds. A pair of bluebirds again began hovering about it the latter part of March the same year our more confiding neighbors reared nine youngsters in the box northeast of the house, though they seemed in no particular hurry to build a nest. Not until the middle of May was the nest built and five blue eggs deposited in it. All the eggs hatched and the young were quite large by the latter part of June, when I placed a blind near the box and secured some pictures of the owners.

I spent considerable time studying the feeding habits of the parents after securing the pictures. The birds made eleven trips to the box with food for the young bluebirds

The more popular of our bird boxes.

in forty minutes one morning late in June, the male making five trips and the female six. They made eighteen trips to the cradle one afternoon early in July from 4:40 to 5:40 o'clock, feeding the young largely upon greenish caterpillars, no doubt cutworms or cabbage "worms," the male making eight trips, the mother ten. That same day, in forty minutes, from 7:05 to 7:45 p.m., they made six visits to the nest, feeding the young two grasshoppers, a spider, a June bug, a beetle, and a batch of tiny red bugs.

The birds made thirteen trips to the nest in thirty minutes one July morning from 8:15 to 8:45 a.m., the male making seven trips, the female six, feeding the young two grasshoppers, two spiders, a batch of tiny bugs, two caterpillars, a large black insect, and other tidbits.

My last glimpse of these birds proved an interesting one. I was returning from the garden one evening, when I heard the youngsters calling for food and found the parents hovering about a near-by fence. I stopped and awaited developments. Soon one of the parents caught an insect and flew to the dead branch of a large black oak, where it fed a young bird. A few moments later the other parent also flew to the branch. I advanced a few steps and counted the birds, finding seven of them perched in a row, so near one another that they occupied less than a foot of space. No doubt they spent the night thus.

I usually see my first bluebird of the year early in March, along about the tenth of the month, or sometimes it may be the twelfth or even the fifteenth. One year, however, he arrived earlier than usual, for it still was February when I first saw him and heard his welcome notes. Thereafter, for several days, I saw nothing of him. Could it have been possible that this bluebird was a scout and that he was up from warmer regions to the south to see if the snow were gone and plenty of food was to be had? He was back again the third of March, however, and quite early in the morning I heard his notes coming from across the fields; but though I frequently heard him all morning I did not get a glimpse of him. Then, about noon, I heard him again, this time about the bur oak near the house. His notes, certainly, were now uttered more freely and had a coaxing or pleading tone, and I soon caught sight of him perched near the top of the tree. I noticed that he lifted, or "twinkled," his wings when twittering, as if very happy, that he had his mate with him, and decided the birds were former neighbors of ours and had nested in our rustic boxes. Each year I make sure that these boxes are secure and in good condition and each year the birds return to them. Eventually the male flew to the favorite box, looked inside, raised his wings, twittered, coaxed, and pleaded until she joined him and also inspected it.

But though the birds early laid claim to their old home they were in no hurry to begin housekeeping. I frequently saw them near the box, into which at times they even carried dead grass for the nest, before they deserted the neighborhood entirely for a long time, so long that I wondered if they were nesting elsewhere. They returned in April, however, and this time began building their cradle in a businesslike way. The first egg was laid on the 22nd of the month and on the 25th the clutch was complete.

Exactly a month later to the day I placed the umbrella blind near the post bird box, to learn what our neighbors were feeding their young. I was sure they were feeding them many cutworms and wished to get some exact information. The four youngsters were now quite large and I noticed that the parents were kept busy early and late feeding them.

The mother fed her young fifteen times the first hour. Five times I saw that she carried cutworms to the nest, while once she had a grasshopper, another time what looked to be a cricket, once a spider with a large egg sac, and finally a white butterfly or moth. Six times I could not see what she had because her back was turned toward me.

The male did not venture near the nest that first hour,

A young bluebird.

and I wondered if he were afraid of the blind or a lazy, shiftless fellow. However, I soon decided he was timid and not lazy, because I heard him uttering sharp notes of alarm as if warning his mate to be careful. "Do you hear me? Do you hear me?" is what he seemed to say.

This male bluebird was quite unlike some others I have known intimately, as I had previously placed blinds near bluebirds' nests several times and had always found the male to be braver and often the harder working of the two. Once, for example, I set the blind near a stump in which a pair of these birds was nesting. The mother never came near the stump while the blind stood near it, though her spouse was equal to the occasion, doing all the feeding and often cleaning house besides.

The mother did all the feeding the second hour also, making twelve trips to the nest with food. Five times I distinctly saw the cutworms she carried, while twice she had grasshoppers, one of which was very large. She went inside the box when feeding the large grasshopper to her young, as if afraid the youngster getting it might choke, or wished to divide it between two or more babies. Five times I could not see what she carried.

Sometimes when flying to the post she looked intently at the blind, making it easy for me to see what she carried, but at other times she turned her back to me and at once fed the young. In the latter eventuality it was impossible for me to see what she had. I tried to attract her attention at such times by pounding upon or shaking the sides of the blind, or waving my pencil just outside the observation hole.

It amused me to see how she carried the cutworms, as she invariably held them by the nape of the neck, much like a cat carries a kitten; and the pests on the whole were very lively and squirmed and wiggled and performed all sorts of aerial, gymnastic exercises with the free parts of their bodies as they tried to break away.

The mother made twenty-four trips to the nest the next two hours for an average of twelve each hour. Eight cutworms disappeared for good during the two hours, as also did two grasshoppers, a butterfly or moth, what looked to be a grubworm, and three or four other insects. Seven times I could not see what she had and the rest of the time I could not identify the pests.

I watched both parents from a distance on the evening of the 26th, and noticed not only that both were working but also that they fed the young until nearly eight o'clock in the evening, or until it was quite dark. The following morning I found the parents feeding their young at 4:30, the mother making two trips in five minutes.

I later spent a fifth hour in the blind near the nest. I knew by that time that Mr. Bluebird was not lazy, but that he was afraid of the blind. However, he overcame his fears enough to feed his young five times, the mother meanwhile making eleven trips, a total of sixteen for both birds during the hour. I concluded from this that the young birds would have been fed a little more often the first four hours if the male had not been afraid of the blind.

From my observations, I concluded that bluebirds feed their young over a period of time of at least fifteen hours each day, and that they feed them about fifteen times each hour, for a total of 225 feedings per day. I spent seven hours and fifty minutes in the blind near the two nests mentioned in this chapter and during that time the parents fed the young 115 times, for an average of 14.7 feedings per hour. I now had some data with which to determine the number of cutworms destroyed daily by our neighbors. I noted the number destroyed the first four hours spent near the latter nest, when 51 trips were made by the mother. Twenty-eight times I could see what she carried, whereas 21 times I could not because she kept her back turned toward me. And 18 of the 28 times, or about two thirds of the time, she had cutworms. Two thirds of 225 gives 150, and from this I consequently estimated that our pretty neighbors fed their youngsters 150 of the pests daily, truly a remarkable performance.

It should be remembered that it is only for their first broods that bluebirds secure many cutworms, and only in places where cutworms are plentiful. Cutworms are most abundant during the months of April, May, and June, so for their later broods bluebirds take other food, in some instances many grasshoppers. Studies made at

Bluebirds at the nesting box.

Washington indicate that about half the bluebird's food in late summer consists of the latter insects. Naturally, bluebirds feed their young seasonable foods. The good work they do is hard to calculate, but we know it is of great importance.

Bluebirds roam about in family parties after the nesting season, the little flocks no doubt consisting of a pair of adult birds and their latest brood. They then lead an easy, carefree life, for they roam wherever their fancies and appetites lead them, gleaning a rich living from the insects to be found everywhere. A bird bath proves highly attractive to them and they are easily lured to the yard by means of one. Some birds begin moving southward again as soon as the nesting season is over, but not so the loved and useful bluebirds. They remain in their northern summer haunts until driven southward by snow and cold weather. Nor do they pack up and leave with the first snow flurry, since it takes a real blizzard and severe cold weather to start them on their southward journey.

Chapter 28

THE ROBIN

OFTEN some experience adds meaning to some well-known saying, proverb, or adage. This is well illustrated by some observations I made of a pair of robins the first day of April one spring. They tended to illustrate or give meaning to the old and familiar words about the early bird being the one to catch the worm. Ordinarily we would interpret this as meaning that the first bird to awake and start out in search of food in the morning is the one that finds and makes a meal of some belated earthworm, cutworm, or other small creature. Now, the fact of the matter is that the early bird is more likely to find and catch earthworms and cutworms, since both are nocturnal, feeding and moving about by night but spending the day safely hidden in the soil. However, all birds are early risers, so all of them have about an equal chance of catching worms and insects slow to seek the safety of the soil before daylight.

But what about the first migratory birds to return to us in the spring: the first robins, bluebirds, meadowlarks, killdeers, and blackbirds; do they also get their worms and insects? What do they find to eat when the ground looks bare and brown, when the snow still covers the north slopes of hills, and when very little green grass and no early wild flowers are to be seen? Does the first robin get his worm? The first bluebird? Meadowlark? If these birds do not find worms or insects, what gives them their sleek and bright-eyed look, what furnishes them with energy, and what enables them to sing so long and sweetly?

Yes, the first spring birds get their worms, although it is not always an easy matter to discover just what worms, insects, and other small creatures they find. A little later, when you see robin hopping, then stopping, looking, listening, and pecking vigorously at the ground, and finding and pulling forth an earthworm, you have the answer to the question. You know robin got his worm and you know exactly what kind of a worm he secured.

Have you ever wondered what the first spring birds find to eat? They return long before insects are to be found in numbers, unless you know just where to look. Take a walk about the time the last snow is disappearing and try to find something that would make a bite of food for a hungry robin or bluebird and you will soon come to the conclusion that were you a bird you would surely starve. But not so the bird. It seems to know just where to look, it has the sharpest of sharp eyes, and no worm or bug is too small, safely hidden, or otherwise protected to escape it.

I was returning from a walk down the pasture on the day in question, carefully choosing a path that would take me from one bare patch of ground to another, since there still was a good deal of snow left from a recent snowstorm. On I went until I discovered a pair of robins feeding on the bare ground. The birds ran or hopped from one pile of oak leaves to another, tossed them aside with their bills, looked carefully beneath them, and found one bite of food after another. What they found was quite large, made no effort to escape, and seemed to taste

very good. How sleek and full of life the birds seemed.
They hurried to a pile of leaves and at once went to work
in a businesslike way, tossed leaves to the right and left,
and found food in abundance. What they found made
them a good mouthful, since they ate each with a gulp.

After watching the birds for some time and seeing
them swallow dozens of bites of food, I decided to see
if I could not discover what they were finding and eating.
And, naturally enough, I decided to search for the insects or other tidbits beneath the leaves. The first insects
I found were some tiny leaf hoppers that went skipping
this way and that from the leaves I moved. I was sure
the robins were not eating many of these little insects,
since the leaf hoppers were too small and full of life. The
birds would have been obliged to chase them and they
would not have eaten them with a gulp. The insects or
other creatures the birds were finding were larger and
less active. Next I found a small black spider that hurried
off and took refuge beneath another pile of leaves. Were
the robins finding and eating spiders? No, I decided
spiders were not what the birds were after, since they,
too, were too small and full of life. Next I discovered a
grasshopper, large enough to make a robin a nice mouthful, but so lively that the birds would have had trouble
catching him. Then, too, there were not enough of them.
I found but one, no more.

I continued my search and soon found a cutworm,
then another, and still another. Soon I had thirteen of
the pests. At last I was sure I had discovered what the
robins had found. Just to make sure, I continued my
search and soon found a dozen more of them, or twenty-
five in all — proving that the robins were eating cutworms. These insects were numerous and large enough to

An incubating robin.

make them a mouthful; they lay still when uncovered from their hiding place beneath the leaves.

Though I now was satisfied I knew what the robins were finding to eat, I decided to make doubly sure. If I could get near enough to the birds, I might actually secure a glimpse of what they were finding and eating. I advanced toward one of the birds, until I was afraid it would fly off if I went any nearer, then stopped and stood perfectly still, watching it. I stood as still as a post for five minutes, ten minutes, fifteen minutes, and noticed that the bird kept getting nearer to me. Soon it was but 15 ft. away, and I saw it eat one cutworm and then another. After that, I stood still, for perhaps ten minutes more, until the bird was but 8 ft. from me and watched it eat another cutworm. I had solved the riddle and learned what the robins were finding to eat. I knew they were finding food in abundance and were doing much good meanwhile. I knew what gave them their sleek, well-fed look, what furnished them with energy, and what made them happy and contented.

Yes, the early birds get their worms. Where the worms are cutworms, so much the better, as these insects are among the worst pests farmers and gardeners have to contend with. Cutworms are the caterpillars of some small but destructive moths. The moths themselves do no harm, but the caterpillars are very destructive, cutting cabbage, tomato, corn, and other tender young plants just above the surface of the ground and forcing gardeners to protect their crops with poison. Bran is mixed with molasses, Paris green, or some other similar poison, and water, and spread about the young plants. This entails much work and considerable expense. By destroying large numbers of cutworms, robins prove themselves to be among the best of feathered friends and neighbors.

Studies made by the United States Department of Agriculture have revealed that 42 per cent of the robin's food consists of animal matter and 42 per cent of wild berries. That leaves a matter of 16 per cent to be accounted for, and here we must admit that our dear friend falls short, for it is fond of cultivated berries and, in taking them, does some harm.

Our robin neighbors usually arrive the second week in March and leave us again in November, though sometimes they arrive earlier in March or late in February, and do not leave in November, at least not all of them, being governed somewhat in their choice of a winter home by the amount of available food and not entirely by the amount of snow and cold weather. There are many hackberry trees to be found in this vicinity, which often are loaded with berries all winter long. And, when these trees have or bear many berries, robins are likely to remain in this neighborhood all winter, living mainly on the berries of these trees. Some years, consequently, I see robins every month in the year, often in flocks, thanks to these stately trees.

Although robins either remain here all winter or return early in March, they are in no hurry to begin nesting, holding off the making of the first nest until April or early May. About my home these birds start a half-dozen nests they never use for one reason or another. I am sure the birds never use some of them because they find after building them that they do not like their locations. Some of them also no doubt are visited by the gray squirrels, of which there are many in the neighborhood, or are built in places where they cannot be anchored properly, or are exposed to the full fury of the wind and rain and are destroyed. But by the latter part of April the wind is not so strong and the birds less fastidious and then they complete nests which they use. Some of these birds have nested, in the vines clinging to our west porch, the past ten or twelve years, often rearing two broods there in a season. Sometimes new nests are built for the second brood, but occasionally one nest is made to do for both, the birds building a new one if they have the time and inclination, otherwise only renovating and repairing the old.

I made a number of robin shelves one spring, hoping to make the premises more attractive to these birds. One of these I fastened to a bur oak southeast of the house, and the remainder to the barn and hen house. These

The nest and eggs of a robin.

shelves have floors 6 by 6 in., are equipped with roofs to keep off the rain, and are open on either two or three sides. They were not used the first two or three years, the birds preferring to build on the branches of trees, in vines, and about our grape and ivy trellises. Eventually the one fastened to the barn wall was used and four young robins successfully reared in the nest built on it. Naturally, I eagerly awaited the return of the birds the following spring, hoping to get an early hint that they intended using one or more of the shelves for their nesting ventures that year. Nor did the birds disappoint me, though they kept me waiting anxiously for weeks before giving me a clue as to their intentions. On the second day of May I noticed that a robin often visited one of the shelves on the hen house. A few days later, when I passed this shelf, I saw that it held a small quantity of grass and weeds. The weather at the time was cold, dry, and windy, and it continued being so for a week, which made the task of building a nest a difficult one, my neighbors working hard for five days without getting it started. They carried grass, weeds, string, and other materials to the shelf, but these were in most instances carried off almost at once by the wind. Sometimes but two or three loads were deposited upon the shelf before a gust of wind carried them off; at other times the foundation would be well started before the inevitable happened.

The birds, I noticed, had a good start the morning of the sixth before the wind carried their materials away. Fortunately, they were not easily discouraged, and on May seventh they had another good start, having a substantial and bulky foundation on the shelf, so I decided to help them if possible. I secured an old oak plank which I leaned against the shelf and tied in place with binder twine, in such a way that the upper end extended an inch or so above the floor of the shelf and held the nest in place. So well did the plank do the work for which it was intended that the strongest wind was not able to dislodge the partly built nest.

I sat down at a distance to see how they would react toward my efforts to help them. Soon the mother arrived with a load of weeds and grass. Apparently she did not notice the plank, for she flew directly to the shelf with her load. On the ninth of the month the nest was ready for use, even having been carefully and neatly lined with soft grass.

Four eggs were laid in the nest in as many days, the last being laid on May 12th. Then incubation began, the mother doing most or all of it, while the male spent most of his time singing sweetly from the neighboring oaks.

The mother proved timid, not at all like many of our robin neighbors. Whenever we went near the hen house, she left her nest and chirped and scolded from the neighboring trees; and when on the nest she was continually on guard, often stretching her neck for a glimpse of us. Any unusual noise also caused her to leave, until we wondered if the eggs would not be chilled. How unlike some other robins I have known intimately this one was. One that nested in a young oak northwest of the house one year was very saucy, screeching and scolding when I went anywhere near her cradle. The feathers on the back of her head stood on end. She often perched 2 or 3 ft. from me and berated me roundly, and sometimes she darted for me, all but striking me on the head as she dashed by. Another one nested in a grapevine beside the porch door and became so tame that I could touch and stroke her when she returned from a foraging trip with food for her young. And never a chirp did she utter no matter how near the nest we got.

About this time another pair of robins began repairing the nest on the shelf fastened to the barn wall, less than 2 rods from the one on the hen house. Soon this nest also was ready for use and two blue eggs were deposited safely in it. Our hen-house robins paid little or no attention to our barn-wall robins, though they often waged war upon a pair of blue jays nesting in a young cottonwood near the house, eventually forcing them to leave.

The nest on the hen house held four young robins on May 26th, and the parents were soon kept busy early and late feeding them. The mother still scolded us when we came near, though she seemed tamer. Before the young birds left the nest, I placed a blind near the shelf and easily secured a number of pictures of her, a thing that would have been impossible two weeks earlier. The young birds grew rapidly and soon were large, bright-eyed, and cunning. They snapped their bills and crouched in the nest if we came too near the shelf to suit them, but quickly relaxed when we left, soon resuming their watchful waiting, expecting at any moment to catch sight of father or mother returning with food for them. On the whole, however, they were unafraid and assumed all sorts of positions in the nest, especially if we remained at a respectable distance. Fourteen days after I first saw them they left the nest, thereafter living for more than a week in the trees near the house.

We also helped a robin that began a nest on the ivy trellis fastened to our west porch one year on the 9th of May. She carried many loads of grass to the site she had selected, but the material did not stay where she placed it, some falling to the ground, the rest being carried off by the wind. The children had been playing with some paper packing in the yard, and this the hard-working bird finally, in despair no doubt, began using. She carried many loads of packing to the trellis, great loads that made her look very queer indeed, since long streamers of the paper often dangled behind her as she flew to the nest. She seemed to be in a terrible hurry, so we did what we could to help her by placing additional quantities of packing about the yard, hanging some on the fence and placing the rest on the ground beneath the trees.

The bird managed to make a good deal of the packing stay in place because of the length of the streamers. We noticed that she squatted and turned this way and that, thus fashioning the materials around her breast, whenever she took a load to the nest; also that she

A nest of young robins.

worked her feet rapidly, as if to pack the streamers tightly together and firmly into place. I estimated that she made about fifty trips to the nest with building material that first day after she began using the paper packing. She began using mud and grass as well and she continued using the packing until the nest was completed. When finished it was white and bulky, with long streamers of paper dangling from it here and there.

But though our robin neighbors built near us, they did not get entirely used to their human neighbors that year and often left their nest and flew off when we went out and in the porch door. And it was surprising how many times a day some of us had to go out or in that door. The eggs no doubt were chilled and but one hatched. The lone youngster grew very rapidly. He was given all the food he could possibly eat and in due time got safely away.

A pair of robins again began loitering around the porch the spring of the following year. The male bird often sang cheerfully from near-by trees, in time being joined by his mate, the two no doubt being the very birds that nested on the ivy trellis the previous year. At least that is what we concluded, since they insisted on nesting near the old site. They carefully inspected the old nest on the trellis, then the vine nearer the porch door, finally choosing a spot 2 ft. north of the screen door in the grapevine. We viewed this with apprehension. Wasn't their choice the height of folly? Would they ever become accustomed to our going out and in the door? The eggs surely would be chilled and the undertaking a failure.

Although this was in March, they often visited the bath and acted as though they knew exactly where they were going to build. But the nest was not started until the 7th of May. Then the birds began gathering grass and carrying it to the chosen spot. The mother, who did practically all the building, then snuggled down upon it and worked her feet rapidly as she packed and wedged it tightly into place. Of course, at first, she worked some of the grass entirely through the tangled vines so that it fell to the ground, though some remained where she wanted it and gradually the foundation was completed. Her feet worked rapidly when actually building, her position changed occasionally, and at times she sat still as if pressing the material into the proper place or shape. The wings were raised and partly spread during the "kicking process," as if to keep the grass from being scattered far and wide by her rapidly moving feet. Occasionally the bird struck a vine or twig with her feet and nearly pushed herself head first out of the nest. That added materially to our enjoyment of the procedure.

The mother made the main part of her nest (the mud bowl) on the ninth, tenth, and eleventh days of the month. No mud was available, as the weather was hot and dry, but the bird was equal to the occasion. She gathered grass, muck, and dirt from the ground, soaked these in the water in the bird bath, then carried them to her nest. Birds certainly are wise creatures. Who can say that they do not use their heads? They know how to get mud for their nests even when none is to be found ready made. Our robins used a good many white chicken feathers that year, perhaps to take the place of the paper packing used the previous one.

We noticed that our neighbors disliked the blue jays that regularly visited the bird bath, often waging war upon them and driving them off, but that they looked with favor upon our chipping sparrows, even allowing a pair of these little birds to nest 7 or 8 ft. from their own cradle, in fact in the very grapevine being used by the larger birds. Our robins also were on the best of terms with some bluebirds nesting northeast of the house.

The first egg made its appearance in the nest on the 12th of May; on the 15th it held four, one being laid each day during the intervening time. The young birds arrived late in May, and after this momentous event I secured some pictures of the mother, who seemed much tamer than at their previous visit. Actually she became so tame that she allowed me to touch her as she brooded the young. Still, at times, during the incubation period, she found it hard to get used to us, often leaving her nest when we went out or in the screen door, until we wondered if the eggs would ever hatch. But all of them did.

The young birds proved very interesting, and I often touched the nest, giving it a slight jar, and watched four little heads, with wide-open mouths, pop up. Their heads and mouths seemed to be operated by springs that were released by slight jars. I noticed, however, that after the mother had fed them that not all the heads and mouths responded when the nest was touched. If a youngster had just been fed his head and mouth failed to respond when the mother next visited the nest. Perhaps, after the next feeding, another head failed to respond, and the youngsters thus no doubt were fed pretty much in turn. We often fed the little fellows, offering them angle-worms and cutworms, and soon learned that the tidbits had to be poked well down their throats. There our offerings apparently touched something that released other springs, for the large wide-open mouths were closed as readily as they formerly were opened.

I well remember the day the young robins left the nest. I took some pictures of them, then fed them some worms I had painstakingly found, and finally tried to secure an additional picture. While adjusting the camera, I touched the vine, shaking it a little, and the little fellows found their wings of service, for away they went. We tried our best to get them back into the nest, hoping to have them with us a few days longer, but all our efforts were in vain. The parent birds had much to do with this, for clearly they chirped and urged and coaxed the young to leave, only being satisfied when they had lured them as far as some trees and bushes four rods west of the house.

But though the young robins were safely out of the nest, we were destined to have them with us for many additional days, for the parents eventually took them to some trees near the berry patch, where our strawberries for many days constituted their staff of life. But they were honest and fearless when securing the berries and visited the patch whether we were there or not. We often picked berries a few yards from a parent robin hard at work doing the same.

Our robins that year proved real bird neighbors, for they not only nested on the house, where they actually lived with us for several weeks, but they remained with us throughout all of the strawberry season and even came back to pay us frequent visits at raspberry-picking time.

Though we did not know it at the time, we were destined to see still more of this pair of confiding birds, for early the next year the same robins, I am quite sure, again began living about the yard. The birds were often to be seen exploring the vines clinging to the porch, as if looking for a place to nest, and several times we were sure they had decided on the place for their cradle. Nevertheless, they seemed in no hurry, and as soon as we were sure they had decided upon a place for the nest, they seemed to desert the neighborhood. Thus things dragged along for weeks, though finally the birds began building upon a trellis, well up under the eaves at the northwest corner of the porch. They could not have chosen a better place and we complimented them on their choice, since the nest was far from the porch door, where the birds would not be disturbed. Then, too, it was well up under the eaves, where it was protected from the rain and hidden from the prying eyes of enemies.

Strangely enough, though we predicted the best of success for our welcome neighbors in their nesting venture, only one of the eggs hatched. However, the parents successfully reared the lone youngster. They led an easy, carefree life the while, because it was an easy matter to supply a single young robin with food. A pair of blue-birds had a brood of four youngsters in a post northeast

This robin faced the camera as much as to say,
"There, take your picture."

of the house at the same time and worked early and
late in their efforts to keep the young supplied with
food. In marked contrast to the overworked bluebirds
were our sleek robins, who never seemed in a hurry and
who took life so easily.

After the young robin had been gone a few days I
noticed an adult robin sitting in the nest under the eaves,
leading me to wonder if the birds were thinking of using
the nest again for their second brood. The next day she
was there again, and the next two also, so I knew our
gentle neighbors were actually using the nest a second
time that year. I climbed to the nest and found that it
held three pretty blue eggs, all of which hatched in due
season. Then our easygoing robins had a harder time
of it.

I sat on the porch one day for an hour and counted the

number of times the birds fed their young. The parents fed the young robins eleven times, or rather made that many trips to the nest with food, both taking turns at the work and father working as hard as mother. The young birds chirped, stretched their necks, and opened their mouths widely for the food brought them. The following day I again counted the number of times the parents fed the young, learning that they made fifteen trips in an hour. I estimated that these robins made at least two hundred trips to the nest each day with food for their young, which accounted for the fact that they now were always busy and had little time for rest, leisure, and song.

That afternoon I noticed that the young robins were getting restless and that they flapped their wings vigorously from time to time for exercise and perhaps to learn if they were strong enough to carry them. Occasionally a youngster stretched and, when so doing, touched or bumped his head against the ceiling of the porch. A few minutes later one little fellow flew off, landing a short distance from the house, after which a second crawled out upon the vine, where he crouched low as if about to try his wings. After crouching a second time away he went, landing about as far from the nest as the first. The third remained in the nest two or three days longer before leaving, and I often saw him when passing the nest, noticing that he usually crouched when he saw me as if trying his best to hide.

Robins have been welcome, pleasant, and real bird neighbors of ours now for more than fifteen years. The final test as to whether birds consider you a friend or an enemy is shown by their confidence in you. They will not nest near you year after year if annoyed or frightened;

but if they feel safe when close by and find things agreeable in other ways, they are likely to continue doing so. There they will be of service to you, and you will be able to enjoy their companionship, listen to their cheerful songs, and learn much by watching them carefully.

Chapter 29

THE GREEN HERON

THE little bird paradise mentioned in Chapter 8, where we photographed the young crows and hawks, is located about 6 miles west of the city of Milwaukee, Wisconsin, and lies between two highways running north and south and lying about ½ mile apart. We spent the greater part of our time within 20 rods of the railway siding, hence nearly all the nests we found were located on a strip of ground 160 rods long and 40 rods wide, which contained about 40 acres of land.

My boy-scout friends and I visited this region regularly for three years; now, so I am informed by one of the boys, it no longer exists, having been claimed by what we call civilization and devoted to the building of homes, shops, and the like. I often asked the boys where they wished to spend the day, and usually they replied that they wanted to visit the "Boxcars"; so to the "Boxcars" we went. Each Saturday and Sunday afternoon and holiday, rain or shine, we were there. If it rained too hard, we took refuge within a boxcar, otherwise we continued our search for birds, birds' nests, wild flowers, and whatnot. We explored the thickets, waded the ponds and marshes, visited the grove, rested, and enjoyed delicious lunches. Sometimes we visited this region of an evening and listened to the songs of the wood thrush and veery and for a time were somewhat baffled by the vesper flight song of the woodcock. We thoroughly cultivated our forty acres, and like any piece of ground that is well cultivated it produced abundantly; crops of birds and nests, however, and not corn, beans, and potatoes. We found scores of nests that had been built by more than twenty species of birds, ranging from the large nests of crows and hawks to the tiny downy cradles of yellow warblers, and including the rare nests of woodcocks, veeries, king rails, and swamp sparrows.

One spring I discovered a large, flat, platform-like nest late in May. It was made of long, slender twigs and located near the top of a young poplar growing near the center of the large thicket located southeast of the sidings. It was the nest of a pair of green herons we frequently found foraging about the shores of the ponds just north of the railway. It was extremely windy the day I found the nest, and the trees swayed and bent until it was a miracle the four light greenish-blue eggs did not roll out of the cradle and fall to the ground.

It then was three o'clock in the afternoon, and the sunlight fell upon the cradle in such a way that excellent pictures of it and the treasures it held could be secured. The nest was in a tree about 15 ft. off the ground, however, too high for photographic purposes. To get worth-while pictures one must get above and to the west of the nest. But how get there? Had there been a large tree standing near the young poplar, the task would have been comparatively easy, since I could have climbed it and worked from a large branch. There were several young poplars surrounding the one in which the nest was located, and these might help, however. But how? I finally selected three whose trunks formed an equilateral

A boy scout interested in birds taking a peep
at the nest of a swamp sparrow.

triangle, and, after pulling their tops together, strapped
them to one another as far up as I could reach. I then
climbed one and strapped the three together a second
time, this time about 12 ft. from the ground. I next
climbed above the upper strap and found that the three
held me up pretty well, especially since I succeeded in
catching hold of the branches of two others and bending
them over the three that supported me. The latter served
a double purpose: they tended to steady me and also they
helped support the camera. I held the lower end of the
tripod legs between my feet and grasped the ball-and-
socket attachment with my left hand, which also held
the tops of the two poplars in place. Between gusts of

The nest and eggs of a green heron.

wind that threatened to send me sprawling head first to the ground, I focused the camera, adjusted the shutter, inserted the film-pack adapter, and made an exposure. I thus took three pictures of the nest and eggs and then left, well satisfied that I would have at least one desirable picture.

The young herons were just out of the shell on June 11th, when I used six crosspieces, each about 4 ft. in length, in making a triangular platform from which to take pictures. The three young poplars used for securing pictures on the previous occasion were used as uprights; three crosspieces were nailed to them 6 ft. from the ground and the others 12 ft. I strapped the camera to the poplar nearest the nest, stood on two of the upper crosspieces, and had little trouble taking pictures of the young birds.

The youngsters were quite lively and continually moved about in the nest, grouping themselves in various cun-

Young green herons in their nest.

ning ways so that I had little trouble securing a half-dozen exposures of them in as many different poses. I visited the place again two days later, but failed to get any additional exposures, since the queer, long-necked, long-legged creatures were livelier than ever and climbed out upon the small branches above the nest, where they either were shaded or too far off for good pictures. I worked for an hour or more trying to get them back into the nest but without success. No doubt, they shortly afterwards left their poplar-tree home.

Each time I visited the place the mother flew off, but in a short time she always returned to the vicinity of the nest, generally perching in a near-by tree, where she sat twitching her ridiculously short tail and sputtering, no doubt trying to tell me what she thought of me. I often stood still at a distance and watched her for a time before advancing and frightening her from the nest, and, on the whole, she did not seem to be very much afraid of me.

Most herons nest in colonies, large numbers of nests often being located near one another, several perhaps in the same tree. The green heron, however, is an exception, as a pair of these birds usually nest here and another there, although sometimes three or four nests are to be found comparatively near together, in the same swampy thicket.

Green herons are our most common ones. They are long-legged wading birds, near relatives of blue herons, egrets, and bitterns, and, though nearly 1½ ft. in length, are one of the smallest members of the family. They are richly dressed during the breeding season, having dark-green crests and backs, reddish-brown necks, and white throats. They are frequently to be seen near the edges of streams and ponds looking for frogs, fish, and other similar tidbits. They fly off a short distance when alarmed, uttering notes of alarm and sometimes seeming to say rather clearly "qui-ick, qui-ick," again squawking harshly.

These small waders are to be seen in most regions boasting a stream, or a few ponds, bordered by thickets, and have escaped gunners by living in scattered pairs. Some herons have been killed in considerable numbers by plume hunters until there are but few of them left, those suffering the most being the ones that live in large colonies and have gorgeous plumes. But the green heron, because less gregarious and gaudy, is still common and, no doubt, if given proper protection, will long continue to be so.

The nest and eggs of a green heron.

I found a green heron's nest in a red-birch thicket on the 5th of June one year. The thicket was on a tongue of land between two large sloughs and, strangely enough, it was less than 80 rods from a city of fifteen hundred inhabitants. However, it was on the west side of a good-sized stream, whereas the city was on the east side, a fact that assured the birds of considerable privacy and enabled them to rear their young without being bothered too much by human beings. The nest held four eggs. It stormed fiercely that night, so I visited the place again the next day, to see how the nest had fared during the storm. I found there were but two eggs left, the others having fallen from the flat cradle during the night, one being broken, the other not.

I placed the whole egg in the grass at the base of the birch and started searching for other nests, soon finding one, also in a young red birch, which held five youngsters only a few days old. I soon found a third, which

Young green herons—"queer long-necked,
long-legged creatures."

also had suffered during the storm, three of its eggs
having fallen to the ground, two of which were broken.
The nest still held a youngster or two and an unhatched
egg. I found another nest about a rod from this one that
held three youngsters that were quite large and who
stretched their long necks in order to watch me. I had
thus accidentally found something a little out of the
ordinary, four green-heron nests near one another, whose
inmates numbered perhaps eight adult green herons and
ten youngsters, or about eighteen in all.

I visited this little colony a few days later and found
that the remaining eggs in the first nest had fallen to the

ground. The mother, however, was not dismayed by the tragedy and soon began laying a number of fresh eggs in the nest, so that, when I last saw it, it held four partly incubated eggs.

Chapter 30

THE KILLDEER

THE killdeer is by far the most common plover to be found about my home. It usually returns from its southern winter home early in March, spending the spring, summer, and autumn with us. We generally hear the first migrating killdeer before we see it, as it flies by high overhead and shrilly calls "kill-dee, kill-dee." Then a glance heavenward usually enables us to see it, a graceful, silvery object high in the sky.

We hear it about the garden and near-by fields for weeks after that, where it calls and flits from place to place while busily feeding upon the stray bits of food it is able to find. It is rather a neighborly bird, seeming to prefer gardens and low-lying, bare fields to grass and pasture lands, no doubt because it is able to find more suitable food in such places.

It becomes noisy when courting and selecting a nesting site, and we frequently hear it at night in May and June, especially if there is a bright moon. It is to be heard at all times of the day also, you may be sure, and there usually are two or more of the birds about. It is an early riser and generally becomes noisy long before the sun rises. It has much work to do and must be up and about its affairs long before most human beings are awake in the morning.

The killdeer nests in fields and gardens, preferably one

plowed, cultivated, and hoed the previous year. The nest is little more than a slight depression in the ground lined with a little grass, a few weed stalks, bits of paper, and the like. But nests have been found that have no lining, the eggs being deposited upon the bare ground. One of the first nests I ever found had been made amid the ruins of a fireworks display in a city park; another, found a few weeks later, had been built in an old watermelon patch. Part of the melons had not been harvested the previous autumn and had been left lying in the field, where they had spoiled, decayed, crumbled until only small bits of crisp, dry rind remained. Amid the ruins of a once juicy and delicious melon the killdeer had built with many tiny bits of rind constituting the cradle.

I find the nests of killdeer in my garden each year and do my best to save them, sometimes leaving small patches of ground about them unplowed, again keeping at a distance when cultivating and hoeing. A nest we tried to save by means of a patch of unplowed ground one spring met with disaster in the end. There were many wind and dust storms that spring, and a particularly violent one struck us about the time incubation was well under way in the killdeer's cradle. Sand and dust swirled about the nest and eggs, completely burying them. I had a stake set near the nest to mark its location, and only by means of this was I able to find any trace of the eggs, for they were buried in 6 in. of sand. I carefully uncovered the eggs, but the mother bird never returned to them.

The killdeer is an expert at feigning injury when you get near its nest, there being several phases to the misleading ruse. At first, when you are at a distance and incubation is not far advanced, it runs off until it finds a suitable depression, all the while uttering shrill "kill-

The nest and eggs of a killdeer.

dee" notes. When it finds a suitable spot, perhaps behind a clod, it squats as if snuggling down upon its eggs, as much as to say: "Look, here I have hidden my nest. See, I am sitting down upon my eggs." Advance, and the bird runs rapidly off until it finds another depression and there repeats the ruse. Both birds of a pair usually take part in this little game of hide-and-seek, one in front, the other farther off.

Get too near a nest when incubation is farther advanced and one or both birds cry "kill-dee," prostrate themselves on the ground, spread their tails until the reddish-brown and other shades show to advantage, spread and flap their wings, and say "dee-dee" in a long rapidly delivered series. Advance a few steps and off they go, crying loudly and soon repeating the performance.

Actually locate the nest and stop to examine it, or work near it, either plowing, planting, cultivating, or hoeing, when incubation is far advanced, and, quite likely, the mother stands up, partly spreads her wings, refuses to move, makes a terrible face, at least so my son insists, and cries out as if in great distress. There are few birds that carry the feigning-injury ruse farther than the killdeer.

"Oh, dear, dear, dear, dear! Oh, dear, dear, dear, dear!" The killdeer whose nest I had just found was terribly upset, running to a depression, squatting, spreading and flapping her wings, and spreading her pretty tail. "Oh, dear, dear, dear, dear! Oh, dear, dear, dear, dear! What a terrible time I am having this morning. I never saw the like before! Oh, dear, dear, dear dear!" The white tips and rust, or reddish-brown, of her tail feathers could plainly be seen, for she was lying on the ground less than a rod from me. Occasionally she rolled over on her side, flapping the opposite wing, rolled over on the other side and flapped the other wing, loudly crying "dee-dee" the while. Although the bird seemed to be badly injured, she carefully kept an eye on me and ran off a few steps when I moved and there went through exactly the same motions again. A killdeer will repeat this ruse a dozen times if you follow it for any distance, and often both birds of a pair will thus feign injury at a distance from each other.

The nest was in the cornfield, 6 ft. from the edge of a piece of unplowed ground, where I had vainly searched for it for two weeks. The nest itself was only a depression in the plowed ground surrounded by a few corn-stalks; it held three eggs one day, and the next four.

The male bird was also in the immediate neighbor-

A killdeer near its nest.

hood, sometimes running beside his mate, more often flying farther off and "dee-dee-ing" and "kill-dee-ing" with all his might.

We were cultivating and hoeing the corn, and, before long, the mother became reconciled to things and returned to her nest, remaining there while the horse, cultivator, and driver passed within a few feet of her. I decided to try to get a picture of her, so set the camera beside the nest, intending to operate the shutter with a string. Soon she was back at the nest, and I walked slowly toward the end of the string, noticing meanwhile that only her head showed and that she was watching me very carefully. She trotted off before I reached the end of the string, and I decided I'd need a longer thread, but soon the horse and driver came along and she hurried to her eggs, while I as quickly ran to the string and secured a picture.

All told I took four pictures of her, although for two of them I was obliged to use a longer string. The four were all secured while the horse and driver were passing the nest and holding her attention, keeping it centered upon the horse, driver, and cultivator and diverting it from the man who was sneaking about the field, trying to get near the far end of a string that was fastened to a queer black contraption standing beside her nest. She was not the least bit afraid of the camera and paid no attention to it.

The four cream-, or buff-colored, eggs are heavily spotted and blotched with black and large for the size of the bird. The youngsters are precocious and follow the parents about as soon as hatched. I sometimes catch sight of one or more of them running about with a parent, the latter carefully watching and guarding them.

One day just a summer or two ago I had an interesting experience of this kind. I was crossing the garden and ran across a killdeer and her young, the mother at once running into a patch of corn with a youngster following her. I followed them but the chick was soon lost to view, no doubt squatting beside a hill of corn, or in a depression, and thus eluding me. I stopped and soon heard a faint "dee-dee" coming from the pasture south of the garden, the notes being uttered by a second youngster coming my way. Occasionally it stopped and bobbed its head in characteristic killdeer style though it was only a few days old. I moved, and the young bird turned and ran to the garden, eventually taking refuge in some tall grass along the north edge, where it squatted and tried its best to hide. I picked it up, held it a few moments, then released it at the edge of the corn, into which it ran and disappeared.

The mother meanwhile was greatly alarmed, flying about me, alighting on the ground, squatting, flapping her wings, and crying loudly, repeating the ruse a dozen times or more. Eventually I started off across the field to the east, and the mother followed me, flew on ahead, dropped to the ground, and dissembled until we reached the line fence 40 rods off. She now flew back to the corn near the garden, quickly made sure her young were safe, then returned and kept an eye on me, circling, calling, and alighting on the ground until I returned to the yard and house, where, to all appearances, she figured I belonged. The killdeer's intelligence, or cunning, is uncanny, unbelievable perhaps, unless you have actually had it for a near neighbor, seen much of it, and had somewhat similar experiences.

Chapter 31

THE MOURNING DOVE

MOURNING doves are accommodating birds, because one is quite sure to see several of them when he is out looking for early bird arrivals in spring; later on, one has little trouble finding two or more nests when he goes nest hunting, even though the nesting season is far advanced. The mourning dove returns to this neighborhood late in March, and nests with youngsters in them are sometimes to be found as late as the 15th of September. And how conveniently the nests are located for photographic purposes! You can nearly always find one on a rail, stump, or branch so near the ground that all you need do is set up the camera and make an exposure, with good results practically assured. Then, too, the nests are shallow so that the eggs show to splendid advantage, and the latter are pure white and always spotlessly clean.

Mourning doves are often to be found in small flocks of a half dozen or more in autumn, gleaning a living of small seeds of various kinds that are to be found abundantly in fields and waste places. The United States Department of Agriculture has found by examining the contents of the stomachs of mourning doves that 64 per cent of their food consists of weed seeds and most of the rest of waste grain. They are among our most effective weed-seed destroyers consequently. They also are among

The frail, flat nest and pretty pure-white eggs
of the mourning dove.

the most numerous of birds, thanks to wise laws passed
for their protection.

I frequently visited a low wooded region along a near-
by stream one spring and summer, where willows and
red-birch trees grew in abundance and were freely used
by mourning doves for nesting. They are not particular
when nesting and will build in most any place boasting
a few trees. Twice I have found these birds nesting in
trees springing from the waters of streams, the flimsy
cradles being less than 3 ft. from the surface. More frequently the birds are to be found nesting in trees leaning
out over the water. One nest that I remember in particular had been built upon a cluster of tiny branches
springing from the trunk of a willow. On the opposite

Young mourning doves.

side, less than a foot away, a pair of grackles had their nest. Mourning doves are peaceful birds; in fact, doves are the symbol of peace; and this may have accounted for the fact that they were able to live in harmony with their dusky neighbors. Most birds would have waged war upon their rivals and either have driven them off or been driven off themselves under the same circumstances. Nor must one give the doves all the credit for this unusual affair, since the grackles were as worthy of praise. I discovered the grackle's nest first and stepped up to it to look at the young birds it held, frightening the incubating dove from her flat cradle when so doing. She fairly tumbled from her nest and went fluttering and zigzagging off through the brush as if injured.

The nest of the mourning dove is made of twigs, weed stalks, and perhaps a few leaves; the two pure-white eggs

A mourning dove brooding her young.

frequently can be seen through the frail structure from beneath. I sometimes find these unsubstantial nests holding two nearly full-grown youngsters and a brooding parent. How the frail affair is strong enough to bear such a load is a mystery, but it generally does, so that one seldom finds either eggs or young birds that have fallen to the ground. The young of many birds look quite unlike the parents, but not so young mourning doves, which have a decided dovelike appearance no matter how small they may be.

As a rule mourning doves are successful when nesting. I once observed seventeen nests from the time they were built until the young left them of their own accord, and all but four of them were fortunate. Two of the ill-fated nests had been built on the ground, and both were destroyed by animals of some kind.

Mourning doves are fully 1 ft. in length, or about as large as cuckoos and bronzed grackles, and are olive

A young mourning dove.

brown in color above but grayish-buff beneath. They have dark spots on the head and wings, and their tails are conspicuously brightened with white.

Their mournful "coo-oo, coo, coo, coo" notes are "soft and ventriloquial" and usually can be heard for no little distance. Sometimes two or more of the birds are to be heard answering or challenging each other, or are they only vying for the favors of the same lady dove? They feed their young on regurgitated food known as pigeon's milk, which is pumped from the crop of the parent into that of the offspring.

I located a mourning dove's nest in a tree along the shore of a near-by stream when out upon a nest-hunting trip by boat one summer. I pulled the boat upon the rocky shore for a look at the young doves, which were nearly full grown. Young mourning doves usually sit still in the nest when intruders come near, though sometimes one flies off a distance. These proved timid and left the nest, one settling on a branch, the other landing in

the water, down which it floated like a little boat. It
floated off as contentedly as a young duck and made no
effort to fly or regain the shore. I leaped into the boat
and hurried after it, soon overtaking it, lifting it into the
boat, and taking it back to the nest. No sooner, however,
had I pulled the boat ashore again than the other
launched forth on its untried wings and also landed in
the water. Then I had another exciting race on my hands.
However, I overtook and rescued it, then brought it back
to the nest. There, after a little petting, both settled down
again, no doubt having decided meanwhile that the nest
was the best place for them after all.

Another mourning dove had her nest in an oak about
20 rods south of the yard one year, in a location I thought
suitable for taking pictures. The cradle was a few feet
out upon a lower branch, too far up for taking pictures
from the ground, so I strapped the camera to the trunk
and attached a string to the shutter release. I then
returned to the yard, from whence the tree was in plain
sight, to await the return of the bird. She came flying
back, edged about a bit, then resumed brooding the young
birds, whereupon I casually made my way by a round-
about manner to the end of the string and released the
shutter. I frightened the bird off, climbed the tree,
changed films, and reset the machine, then returned to
the yard again. Once more the bird returned to her
duties and I secured another exposure, this time a back
view, after which I removed the machine and allowed
the bird to brood her young in peace.

Chapter 32

THE BOBWHITE

"BOBWHITE," or "bob-bob-white," is the song of the bobwhite, or quail, a charming bird song I often hear coming from across the field and pastures. "He-eer" is the call of this bird, and when I hear it coming from scattered places in the neighborhood I know that a number of the birds have become separated from the main flock and are trying to locate their companions. Often, when out for a walk, I hear other characteristic bobwhite sounds, explosive "whirrs" that startle me. Each "whirr" is made by a frightened bird that bursts from the grass or brush near me and goes hurtling off like a feathered bombshell.

Although we have lived a long time in a region where bobwhites are numerous, we never had them for close winter neighbors until only a few years back. To be sure, we often saw and heard them previous to that, but they never made their home about the premises, although an occasional pair nested near the house. Our chubby bird neighbors moved into the vicinity early in autumn and lived near us all winter, their favorite refuge and roosting place being a large brush pile in the pasture. They always flew to this place when frightened from the yard or grove, where they waited until the coast was clear, then returned to their favorite foraging ground. Sometimes, when working near the brush pile, I frightened

The nest and eggs of a bobwhite.

them from it, but they generally returned to it as soon as I was safely on my way again.

Bobwhites live on a variety of food: waste grain, grass seeds, weed seeds, acorns, insects (notably the Colorado potato beetle), and other things they find. One day a large flock of sparrows was feeding upon weed seeds in a small field south of the barn. I watched the little gleaners for some time and eventually noticed that they were hurrying toward a group of bobwhites. Soon the two flocks joined, and the sparrows and quail fed for a long time near one another, traveling leisurely from one patch of weeds to another. The bobwhite is famous for eating weed seeds, which make up more than 50 per cent of its food.

Bobwhites are fond of acorns, and it was great fun to

watch when they were eating them. They ran from the base of one oak to that of another, pecked vigorously at acorns, picked up tiny bits of acorn kernels wasted by the squirrels and redheaded woodpeckers, and seemed as fond of the nuts as children of candy.

Bobwhites usually travel from place to place afoot, sometimes walking but more often running as fast as they can. If possible, they travel from bush to bush, tree to tree, or from one thicket or patch of weeds to another. They run rapidly and are constantly on their guard when in the open, but are less cautious when near shelter, walking slowly and often cuddling down on the sunny side for a rest and a sun bath. They hold their heads high but allow their tails to droop when running; and they move their feet surprisingly fast, so fast, I am tempted to say, that all you see of them is a blur. Although their steps are short, they get over the ground remarkably quick.

I had three ways of keeping track of my chubby bird neighbors that winter. Naturally, in the first place, I saw them almost daily. Secondly, I often heard them calling "he-eer, he-eer" to one another when separated, exactly as if saying, "Here I am, where are the rest of you?" At other times I neither saw nor heard them, but knew where they had wandered and what they had been doing by the tracks they left in the snow. One day, for example, I heard them calling, and, upon looking out through a south window, saw two beside an oak near the barn. Where were the rest and what were they doing? I found the snow south of the barn covered with tracks when I went outside later and thus learned that those I did not see had been in the barnyard hunting food. I also learned that all of them had made a leisurely journey to the oak

The favorite refuge for our first bobwhite neighbors.

grove for acorns, when on my way to town two days later, seventeen trails in the snow telling me the whole story.

There were but thirteen of the birds when the flock first began living in the neighborhood, and one of these was killed by an automobile in a near-by street. Then, all at once, the number increased to seventeen. Where did the five additional birds come from and why did they join the larger flock? Did they once belong to a flock numbering eighteen or twenty, and were the others killed by hunters or destructive animals? Perhaps the five became so hopelessly separated from their former companions they lost all track of them and joined those living near us. Was there any quarreling when they joined the larger flock, and how did they affect the combination? To these and many other questions I should like to learn the answers.

A large hawk was frequently to be seen in the neighborhood late that winter. He usually perched in a tree where he had a good view of its surroundings, and now and then flew about the vicinity in search of prey. Eventually it stalked, killed, and ate one of the bobwhites. It no doubt got others also, although I have positive proof of but one tragedy. We had many bobwhite neighbors the next few winters also, though I have nothing unusual to record, the birds roaming about the thickets near the yard, the oak grove, pasture, and fields, and gleaning a living of weed seeds, waste grain, and acorns.

The weather turned very cold and stormy one year during the third week of January, whereas it had been mild until then, the thermometer registering ten degrees below zero a few times but no more. It remained bitterly cold for five long weeks, the mercury often sinking to twenty or more degrees below. A bevy of bobwhites began visiting the fence row and grape trellis east of the house late in January, no doubt in search of food, and we decided to try to help them, shoveling the snow from the ground diagonally across the yard. One end of the bare patch was near the east living-room windows, the other near an evergreen beside the grape trellis. We shoveled the snow from beneath the evergreen also, giving the birds a place to hide and secure shelter from the cold and wind. We then scattered corn, crumbs, suet, and acorns on the ground from which we shoveled the snow.

The next time the bobwhites visited the yard they fed from the feeding place we had prepared for them. Nor were they alone, for a half-dozen blue jays, several Eng-

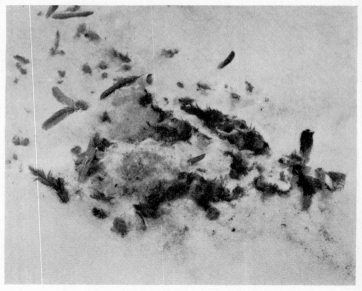

Where a large hawk killed a bobwhite.

lish sparrows, some juncos, a tree sparrow, and a cardinal came also.

It snowed all day the third of February, and the bob-whites sank so deeply into the light, fluffy snow when they came for their evening meal that only their heads could be seen. They were obliged to fly and not walk or run, as they generally do, to make any headway at all, but one reached the feeding place eventually, upon which 2 or 3 in. of snow had fallen since we cleaned it that morning. It ran here and there, eagerly looking for food, but found none. Finally it began to scratch, however, and at once found a kernel of corn. Six others now arrived and were not slow to take the hint, at once beginning to scratch and find food.

We loved to see them twirl their tails, rise on tiptoe, and flap their wings, as if full of life and good spirits, but were surprised to notice how frightened they became when they caught a glimpse of any of us. Then they stretched their necks, uttered notes of alarm, spread their tails, and dashed for the evergreen and grape trellis, or took to their wings and flew farther off. If one secured a kernel of corn, others tried to take it from him; and they jostled one another in order to get a choice morsel or secure a good scratching place. When eating large kernels, they picked them up several times until they got them in the best position for swallowing, then gulped them down, thrusting the head sharply forward two or three times during the process. Their appetites satisfied, they took refuge beneath the evergreen or grape trellis, where they huddled in a group and rested. The more we saw of them the more we marveled at their similarity to domestic hens.

The jays and English sparrows flocked to the feeding spot when they saw the bobwhites at it, as if afraid the larger birds would get more than their fair share of the food. The bobwhites, however, were boss and forced the smaller birds to keep out of their way. The jays carried off much of the corn I threw outside at first, but I learned to outwit them by throwing the corn into the snow along the edge of the cleared spot, where they had trouble finding it. The bobwhites, on the other hand, climbed the snowbank, ran their heads into the snow, scratched, and had little trouble securing the food.

The number of bobwhites varied from time to time. There were fourteen of them at first; then, one day, something frightened them and they scattered in all directions, one flying against a window screen. There were but fourteen of them for some time after that, though later the number increased to twenty-two and finally to about forty.

A large hawk lived for a time in the neighborhood that winter also. Once, perhaps twice, it swooped over the bare spot of ground, sending the bobwhites scurrying in all directions, as if a bombshell had been thrown into their midst.

"I just returned to my typewriter from the front room, where I spent the past twenty minutes watching a number of bobwhites feeding from a bare spot in the yard. This morning, before it was light, I scattered some corn there for our bird neighbors, but now all the food has disappeared. There were but two bobwhites in the yard when I first stationed myself at the window, but additional ones kept coming from the corncrib and barnyard until there were fifteen, the birds settling in the snow a rod off, then running to the feeding place, where they saw their comrades were finding something to eat. They already have been out there three or four times today, the first time just as it was getting light this morning.

"They ran here and there and quickly gobbled a few bites as soon as they reached the bare spot, then settled down to feast more at their leisure, scratching vigorously in the snow like a hen in straw, occasionally wagging and twirling their tails, healthy, alert, contented.

"We watch the birds from the front room because we can hide behind the lace curtains and watch them without being seen, and, though the curtains screen us from their sharp eyes, we have no trouble watching our delightful neighbors through them. And are the chubby birds sharp eyed! They are sure to see us and run off if

Tracks in the snow made by bobwhites.

we try to watch them without hiding behind a screen of some kind.

"We began feeding the birds late in the season, on the tenth day of January to be exact, as the weather previously had been mild with little snow. On the morning of the 8th of January we found the ground covered with about 10 in. of snow; it had turned bitterly cold by the tenth, so we prepared to feed our bird neighbors, shoveling the snow from a spot of ground about 7 ft. in diameter and scattering corn and other food about it. We placed a food tray near an east window, supplied it with crumbs and oatmeal, and tied a piece of suet to a stick at one corner. That day a flock of English sparrows, a cardinal grosbeak, about a dozen blue jays, and fifteen bobwhites were out there at one time or another; all reappeared on the eleventh, with an additional cardinal, and a starling; and today a tree sparrow joined the contented company.

"We also shoveled the snow from the ground beneath a red cedar that stands about a rod from the food tray, connecting this with the feeding place by a path. The bobwhites go to the cedar and huddle in the sunshine after finishing their meal, or run to it and hide when frightened, being there now as I write. I can distinctly hear them calling 'he-eer he-eer' occasionally, as much as to say: 'Here we are. Where are the rest of you?' since they are trying to locate some of their missing companions."

Thus ran the summary I found in my notebook for the 12th of January, a few years back, telling how we came to have bobwhite guests that winter and giving you a glimpse of a peaceful domestic scene and the opening events in a story that ended in tragedy for some of them.

The blue jay is good for something, being an expert at discovering dangers and enemies, crying in a loud voice, dashing off and taking refuge in some safe place, and putting other birds on their guard. I heard a blue jay crying loudly at about 2:30 in the afternoon on the 14th of January, and glancing out through a south window caught a glimpse of it as it flew rapidly northward. I next glanced toward the corncrib, where I had noticed a number of bobwhites a few minutes earlier, but saw none. Where were they? I concluded they were hiding beneath the crib, which clears the ground by about a foot and is supported by two concrete abutments, one at either end.

Just then a large hawk came flying around the corner

of a shed that stands less than 10 ft. east of the crib, at once dropping to the ground and dashing beneath the latter. Out came the bobwhites on the other side, as if sent flying in all directions by a very fierce explosion, closely pursued by the hawk, the latter stopping, rising to its full height on the ground, and looking defiantly about. There was a wicked gleam to the eyes of the bold marauder; it lifted and adjusted its wings and opened and closed its beak; and it seemed puzzled, as if asking: "Now, what on earth became of all those bobwhites?"

I secured a sixteen-gauge shotgun and hurried outside, hoping to get a shot, but by the time I reached the yard the hawk was nowhere to be seen. I hurried to the corn-crib but found nothing there, not even a feather, indicating it had not so much as touched a bobwhite. The hawk's eyes were unaccustomed to the dim light beneath the crib and this perhaps proved of advantage to the bobwhites; then, too, the crib is so near the ground the hawk was forced to alight before dashing beneath it, and this, too, was of help to our chubby neighbors, for a hawk strikes with its feet, which it can do most effectively when on the wing, falling upon its prey like a thunderbolt.

One of the bobwhites flew against a kitchen window with a loud thud in its mad flight to elude the hawk. It was sitting in the snow beside the foundation when I stepped outside, from whence it flew with whirring wings. It had not been injured apparently.

"Why, the nerve of that hawk!" exclaimed my wife. She was sitting near an east window watching some bobwhites feeding from the bare spot in the yard. All told, there now were twenty-three of them, eight having joined the flock since earlier in the month.

I hurried to the window, at once discovering four bobwhites lying on the ground, eyes wide and bright, not a feather nor eyelid moving, two near the center of the cleared patch, two near the snow at the edge. Glancing toward a bird box fastened to a post about 2 rods northeast of the birds on the ground, I saw the hawk perched upon it, eyes blazing, opening and closing its beak and adjusting its wings in characteristic style. As quickly and stealthily as possible, I secured the gun and hurried to the yard, but failed to get a shot, the marauder again having completely vanished as if swallowed by the earth. The bobwhites were still lying motionless upon the ground when I returned to the living room — they seemed to realize the hawk could not see them so long as they remained motionless. Their protective colors concealed them, and they continued to lie there without making a single move for fifteen or twenty minutes longer, then resumed their interrupted meal. They had escaped death by a narrow margin, and soon overcame their fears.

I returned to the yard to ascertain the whereabouts of the others, frightening about a dozen from beneath a grape trellis near the bird box upon which the hawk had perched; these flew to a bushy Russian mulberry tree about 4 rods off, where they joined several others. I concluded all had escaped the hawk again.

It snowed and drifted that night, forcing us to get out early and shovel snow from the feeding place. The bobwhites were hard on our heels, coming flying and running before we had even succeeded in throwing any corn outside. They ran briskly over the ground, eager, expectant, searching but finding little or no food, so began to scratch. And how they did scratch! exactly as if they realized they must fill their crops as rapidly as possible. That terrible hawk might come dashing along any minute, and tomorrow they might be obliged to go hungry. I decided to try throwing some corn among them, as I had done once or twice the previous winter, crouching, sliding, and worming my way along the living-room foundation, where I was screened from view by the corner of the house and two sprawling junipers. I reached the desired spot and threw four handfuls with all my might toward the birds, though I could not see the effect of my efforts. Did the birds become frightened and run off or did they remain and eat the corn? When I returned indoors, I was told the birds actually ran my way when it suddenly began to rain corn, pouncing upon the kernels as soon as they struck the ground. Encouraged, I repeated the ruse with the same result.

It was bitterly cold on the 23rd of January (23 degrees below zero), when the bobwhites arrived for their breakfast before it was fully light in the morning. The flock still numbered twenty-three, thus giving us twenty-three bobwhite guests on the 23rd of the month when the thermometer registered 23 degrees below zero! The birds fed in a compact group, squatted, fluffed out their feathers, ate slowly, and seemed sluggish from the cold. Eventually they ran to the grape trellis and sat in a huddled group for a long time. They had considerable frost about their feathers; and we could see how they had kept their heads covered and warm, as tufts of feathers, held in place by frozen vapor from their breath, stood out where the head had been held.

Chapter 33

MORE ABOUT THE BOBWHITE

GRADUALLY, but very gradually, it must be admitted, the bobwhites seemed to be getting tamer, running around the buildings, along the fence, and sometimes wandering to the garden after weed seeds. When they saw any of us at a window or in the yard, they stretched their necks, lowered and spread their tails, and looked very alert and alarmed, and ran as fast as they could to the cedar and grape trellis. We affectionately called them "our bobs," though we sometimes changed this to "little dummies" when they insisted on remaining shy and timid.

Here are some lines from my notebook for the 29th of January that show that they changed their ways and became wilder again, perhaps because they had been molested by the hawk: "Our flock has increased to twenty-nine, there being that many bobwhites at the feeding place this morning. They seemed to be suffering from a bad case of nerves, for they stampeded and flew to the trellis before they had gotten well started eating their breakfast. Poor, frightened bobwhites! Every moment of the day they must be on their guard or be killed and eaten."

On the 1st of February I added the following: "When we first began feeding our birds we fully expected the bobwhites to get tamer and tamer as the weeks passed, but, instead, find that they are getting wilder. When they come for food, they run rapidly until they reach the bare spot, quickly gobble a few bites, then hurry back to the cedar. If they catch a glimpse of us, they stretch their necks, lower and spread their tails, and run as if their lives are in danger, as they are, but not because of us. Sometimes all take to their wings, there apparently being an explosion of birds, fly to the grape trellis, where they join some of their even more timid comrades that have not yet mustered enough courage to come at all.

"Sometimes all twenty-nine of the birds take off and fly to a favorite brush pile across a road located 20 rods to the south, or to a bushy mulberry standing near the edge of a thicket a few rods to the north, where they doze and rest until hungry again. They seem so sleek and full of life that I am wondering if they are not wild because we feed them too much. No doubt they have considerable fat stored about their plump little bodies and would get through the rest of the winter without any help from us. Little wonder, they are wild, when they are so well fed. Food is not something to be gotten at all hazards, as it ordinarily is during severe winter weather, hence were we to neglect them for a few days they might regain their appetites and be less wary."

On the 8th of February I wrote: "Yesterday I noticed that apparently all twenty-nine of our bobwhites were sitting in a circular group beneath the bushy mulberry north of the house. Just to make sure, I decided to count them when they came for their supper, supposing that the birds would leave by ones, twos, and threes, walking or running to the grape trellis and cedar and thence on to the feeding place. I was mistaken in my supposition. All at once several broke away, ran a few steps, then took

A winter roosting place of bobwhites.

to their wings, the rest following them almost immediately. And no sooner did they reach the trellis and
cedar than they rushed to the feeding place like a squad
of football players, taking it by storm and gulping and
gobbling until there was little corn left; and no sooner
had they eaten a dozen kernels or so each than they hurriedly returned to the cedar. I managed to count them as
they ran off and found there were twenty-eight. They did
not tarry at the trellis either, but at once flew back to the
mulberry, reaching it, I estimated, less than five minutes
after leaving it. I am still hoping to get a picture of the
birds, but how I am going to manage it if they keep on
being shy and gulping their meals I do not know. I

suppose I'll have to feed them less corn, forcing them to scratch and spend more time at the feeding place.

"Toward evening we saw a lone bobwhite sitting beneath the cedar — the twenty-ninth member of the flock — the white patch on the throat proclaiming the sex and indicating he soon would be whistling that clear 'bobwhite' of his, or is it 'more-wet'? or 'more bites,' as some fishermen insist? We tapped on the window, but he paid no attention to us. Was he ill? I opened the window and he at once stood up, stretched his neck, spread his tail, and ran to the trellis. Later he came to the bare spot and ate some corn. Apparently he is the tamest of the flock."

February ninth: "The lone bobwhite returned this morning. How hungry he was! I watched him eat his breakfast. I had always supposed a dozen kernels of corn would make a bobwhite a hearty meal, but this fellow actually ate thirty-five before flying off. Bobwhites must have large crops. Thirty-five kernels of corn to one meal! Take that many large kernels of corn, hold them in your hand, and you will get an idea of how much food a bobwhite can eat at a time."

At about nine o'clock the morning of the 14th of February I heard a blue jay scream loudly again. It had discovered danger as usual and was clamorously voicing its alarm. One of our bobwhites dashed toward the corn-crib, while another uttered a peculiar cry I never before had heard. A moment later that bloodthirsty hawk came flying around the corner of the house, dropped to the crusted snow near the garage, and I saw it had a bobwhite in its claws. It looked my way, and it seemed as if its piercing eyes were actually ablaze. I quickly secured the gun — it was standing almost within arm's reach — and returned to the window to find the hawk had vanished, so ran outside, hoping to get a shot, but it was nowhere to be seen.

My first impression was that the hawk dropped upon the bobwhite at the corner of the garage, but I have since concluded it pounced upon it at the feeding spot, carried it to the garage, and stopped there to secure a better grip upon it. As to the peculiar cry, I am quite sure this was an alarm note, although it is possible it was the death cry of the stricken bird. We were destined to hear that cry again, a cry that caused us to experience a most peculiar feeling, a mixture of alarm, horror, anger, as if our children were being killed before our eyes. If the hair on the back of a person's neck ever stands on end, I am sure mine did when I heard that frightened, panicky, appealing cry. How sorry we felt for the poor little bobwhites we had learned to love and whose companionship we enjoyed so much.

I noticed that the bobwhites did not follow their long-established custom of feeding in the early morning that particular day. It seemed to me they realized there was winged death abroad, or had they caught an early glimpse of the hawk and hesitated to leave their roosting place because of the look? Only three or four new birds came, and it was one of these the hawk killed. Late in the afternoon the main flock came, and I counted the chubby birds as they ran briskly off, finding there were thirty-one of them, the twenty-nine we had been feeding and two of those feeding in the yard when the hawk swooped; or was the lone male bobwhite still absent and the enlarged flock composed of the other twenty-eight and the three survivors of the morning's tragedy? Not only did the birds come late in the day to feed instead of early in the morning, but they went off in a different direction after they had had their supper, perhaps with the idea of spending the night in a new place. Birds that roost on the ground must change their roosting places often, otherwise they are likely to fall a prey to rats, weasels, foxes, and other predatory animals. Bobwhites do this, no doubt, for the roosting places I run across clearly show that most of them have been used for only a few nights. Our chubby neighbors flew off across the fields to the east and southeast after they had had their supper later in the winter, no doubt roosting in two large brush piles we could see from the house.

We predicted the hawk would be back in a day or two, upon the assumption it would not soon forget about the delicious meal it had just secured. Nor were we mistaken, for I frightened it from an oak in the grove when I stepped outside to go to town for the mail the next morning, the bird flying on to another near the drive, within shooting distance I judged. I secured the gun, shot, but failed to get it, either because my aim was poor or the distance too great, most likely the latter, for I was not excited and aimed very carefully. Off the marauder went, but settled in a tree at the far end of the pasture, from whence it hastily flew when it saw me coming down the drive.

Naturally, I do not shoot at a hawk without weighing arguments pro and con as to the justice of so doing, though in this instance there could be few or none against shooting. Most authorities hold that the proper way to handle the hawk problem is to shoot only those actually caught doing harm and to let the rest alone, a procedure I believe to be wise and scrupulously follow. Most hawks are highly useful because of their feeding habits, destroying many insects, gophers, rats, and mice each year,

The cedar that figures in the story of our bobwhite
neighbors after a heavy snow.

though a few species are destructive and some of the useful ones sometimes get into bad habits.

The weather now turned mild, the snow began to melt,
and many were the signs of spring to be observed on the
18th, 19th, and 20th days of the month. The weather,
however, was too nice to last; such warm periods usually
are "weather breeders," and, in winter, are likely to be
followed by rain or snow, strong winds, and colder
weather. We had a few showers on the 20th, and, toward
night, it began to sleet and then to snow heavily, the
wind blustering and roaring all night long. The storm
continued all the next day and the fields and woods were
badly drifted by night. It was partly cloudy and still

windy the 22nd, when we dug ourselves out of the worst storm of the year. The first snow that fell on the 20th was soft and moist, clung to the trees, wires, branches, and other things, and froze so securely in place that little had been dislodged by the wind by the 22nd. Branches bent beneath the snow, bushes sprawled, and two red cedars in the yard were bent double, while the snow was dazzling white and the outdoors a sparkling fairyland.

The hawk returned on the 22nd and seemed bolder than ever, no doubt because it was extremely hungry, having found little to eat during the period of warm weather, when the bobwhites and other birds had fed about bare spots of ground where they were concealed by their protective colors. It settled in a box elder southeast of the house, some blue jays at once giving the alarm. The hawk took after the jays, hopping clumsily from branch to branch, striking and killing one, the stricken bird falling and disappearing in the snow. The hawk now flew to the shed, then back to the box elder, while I secured the gun with the idea of shooting it through the window. Unfortunately, I could not open the window the first try, the sleet and ice holding it, and, when I did, it flew open with a bang that frightened the hawk away.

We did not see the bloodthirsty marauder again until the 1st of March, when we again heard the alarm notes of the bobwhites. I ran to the window and at once caught sight of the hawk in pursuit of a lone bobwhite it had frightened from beneath the cedar or trellis. Off the two raced southwards, down into a hollow, up over a rolling hill, across the road, on toward some brush piles ¼ mile distant, the hawk gaining, gaining, gaining, until it seemed it must surely overtake its prey. It was a nip-and-tuck race and we were wild with anxiety for the bobwhite. I could not determine the outcome of the race from the house, whether life or death had been the final outcome, so started off across the field, gun in hand. When halfway to the brush piles, the hawk flew from a small bur oak in which it had settled, flying eastward, the bobwhite no doubt having escaped it. Relieved, I returned to the house. In so doing I made a mistake. I should have hunted that hawk as relentlessly as it was hunting the bobwhites, not stopping until I had succeeded in killing it.

The hawk did not get the bobwhite, that we knew with absolute certainty in the afternoon, when we again heard that heartbreaking cry in the yard. Had it eaten its fill in the morning it would not have been so hungry and bold in the afternoon. The cry sent us rushing to the windows, where, at first, we looked in vain for both the bobwhites and the hawk. Finally, I chanced to glance toward the grape trellis, where the bobwhites had spent much of the morning, both before and after the wild chase across the fields. I saw something in the snow beneath the trellis but could not tell exactly what it was because of the dense, tangled grape vine. A moment later I saw it was the hawk, which came tumbling out, trying to use its wings and dragging a bobwhite. I grabbed the gun, slammed the window open, leaped outside, ran in the direction I thought the hawk had taken but failed to find a trace of it. As usual, it had disappeared as if swallowed by the earth, flying near the ground where it was screened by bushes, trees, and hills. I walked for some distance northward, hoping to find it either in a tree or on the ground devouring its prey, but failed. As I neared the house on the return journey I learned it had also killed and eaten a bobwhite beneath the bushy mulberry, a few

An ill-fated bobwhite's nest—a wide strip of unplowed ground was left around it and the eggs disappeared one by one.

bones, some blood spots, and a great mass of feathers telling the whole story. The toll of the hawk thus leaped from one to three. Winged death was abroad, one extremely hard to cope with, and I sincerely hoped the weather soon would turn mild and the snow disappear, so our chubby neighbors could make full use of their protective colors.

March ninth: "Only once have we seen our chubby neighbors since the 1st of March, the date of the final gruesome tragedy, for they have not come to the yard for food since. There are three reasons for this: (1) they no doubt realize they are being relentlessly hunted by that hawk and must change their foraging grounds or

perish; (2) we stopped feeding the birds, since we realized we were luring them to their death so long as we
were unable to shoot the hawk; and (3) the snow melted
rapidly the first week of the month, the bare spots becoming larger and natural food more plentiful and easily
secured. We could not help wondering if the bobwhites
thought we offered them food, lured them to the yard,
and then turned that bloodthirsty hawk upon them. If
so, how can they ever trust us again or feel safe when
near the house? I doubt if they reasoned about the matter
at all, though they do know that the feeding place, trellis,
and bushy mulberry are dangerous places, spots to be
avoided, hence they stay away. I frightened several of
them from a heap of dry, brown leaves beneath some
brush in the pasture on the 6th of March, the birds flying
off with loudly whirring wings and startling me as they
always do. I was thankful most of them had escaped the
hawk, but could not help wishing I knew exactly how
many the killer got, for it must have taken others than
the three it secured in the yard. Also, I am wondering if
any of them are likely to nest near us, as I was sure some
of them would before the hawk made its appearance."

We did not see much of our bobwhite neighbors the
following winter, though we did see the hawk from time
to time, either flying by or perching in a distant tree.
Two years later the chubby birds returned to the yard
early in December and remained with us until February,
when the denouement came with startling suddenness.
We had not seen a sign of the hawk and it was far from
our thoughts, when, one cold day, the blue jays loudly
voiced their alarm, thereby telling us an enemy of some
kind was about, either a cat or a hawk. I glanced out
through an east window and at once discovered the

cause — that hawk perched on a wren box hardly a rod from the feeding place. I quickly secured the gun, ran out the back door, and wormed my way along the living-room foundation until I reached the spot from which I had thrown the corn among the bobwhites two years earlier. Stealthily, screened by the junipers and corner of the house, I edged forward, gun cocked and in position for shooting, until the sight rested on the marauder, and shot. The hawk fell less than 8 ft. from the base of the cedar. Out came a dozen frightened bobwhites from beneath it, uttering that appealing, startled, panicky cry as they hurried off. One struck the corner of the house, glanced to the snow near my feet, then took to its wings and flew on again. There they had been hiding beneath the cedar, well aware that winged death was perched less than 6 ft. away, almost above them. We saw little of them for about a week, but then they came timidly back for a bite to eat, feeding beneath the window one day, being gone the next, gradually resuming their former habits.

The hawk was nearly 20 in. in length, had a wing spread of 42 in., was dark brown above, barred with other shades, much lighter underneath, barred and streaked with brown, had white bars across the tail, a bluish beak, and was distinctly reddish-brown about the shoulders — a red-shouldered hawk that had fallen into evil ways.

INDEX